I0874926

delta

delta

KERRIE DAVIES

A Sue Hines Book
Allen & Unwin

The author is donating a share of the royalties from this book to the Australian Red Cross and to the Aids Trust of Australia.

First published in 2005

A Sue Hines Book
Allen & Unwin
83 Alexander Street
Crows Nest NSW 2065
Australia
Phone: (61 2) 8425 0100
Fax: (61 2) 9906 2218
Email: info@allenandunwin.com
Web: www.allenandunwin.com

National Library of Australia
Cataloguing-in-Publication entry:
Davies, Kerrie, 1972- .
Delta.
ISBN 1 74114 548 1.
1. Goodrem, Delta. 2. Women singers – Australia – Biography. 3. Television actors and actresses – Australia – Biography. I. Title.
782.42164092

Cover and text design by Nada Backovic
Typesetting by Pauline Haas
Edited by Jennifer Castles
Printed in Australia by McPherson's Printing Group

10 9 8 7 6 5 4 3 2 1

Contents

"I am living the dream I've wanted since I was a little girl."

Delta

CHAPTER 1

Bring It On

On a sweltering summer's evening, 20,000 people sprawled on the grass outside Parliament House in Federation Mall, Canberra to celebrate 'Christmas in the Capital'.

Some of the biggest names in Australian pop music were performing at the outdoor concert, but there was one girl everyone was waiting for as the sun set. Children wearing glow-in-the-dark antlers strained on their parents' shoulders, cooled by Parliament House sprinklers that had gently been turned on earlier in the evening to relieve the unrelenting heat.

When she appeared on the stage, an adoring roar floated into the sky. She smiled and waved, then settled at the antique German piano and fidgeted with her stiletto shoes. Behind her, Parliament House was eerily lit up with garish images of moons and rainforests, but she didn't need the adornment. Unlike earlier artists, Delta commanded the audience's attention with just her presence.

There was silence for a moment, a feeling of anticipation and admiration for the teenager whose gutsy ballads had entranced Australia. Elegant and classy, eighteen-year-old Delta was dressed in a sparkling, sophisticated black halter-neck for the Christmas performance. Shiny black earrings dangled from her ears as she bent over the piano. Her hair was groomed straight, her make-up perfect, her voice powerful and clear.

Delta had the No. 1 single in the country, was a TV star and a teen idol. As she sang her hit *Born To Try*, the crowd dreamily waved along. Then Delta sang some traditional Christmas carols like *Silent Night*.

The applause and screams for Delta were still filtering through to backstage when fan Rachael Ward slipped around the door to meet with Delta and get her autograph. Rachael's mother,

"It's **all** good."

Delta

Julie Ward, had produced the concert and Rachael had been waiting all night for her chance to meet the performer.

But as she approached Delta and her mother Lea, she was amazed to see a very different person to the composed, confident star she had seen on stage earlier that night. The singer was distraught and being comforted by Lea. She had missed the high note in *Silent Night*, and couldn't forgive herself.

'She was sitting with her mum at a table and all upset because of missing the note,' recalls Rachael. 'I told her not to worry, she was my favourite singer by far. She said I was an angel, and very sweet. One day I want to be a singer, just like her. She is my idol.'

The shy fan, with modest words of reassurance to her crestfallen idol, had just seen the public and private worlds of Delta Goodrem collide.

In public Delta's life is, to quote one of her favourite sayings, 'all good'. Since releasing *Born To Try* three days before her eighteenth birthday, Delta has become one of Australia's biggest selling artists. Her debut album *Innocent Eyes* sold 2.5 million copies and has gone platinum fourteen times. Her second album, *Mistaken Identity*, debuted triple platinum. To date she has had eight consecutive No. 1 releases. She has won a record-breaking seven ARIA awards, a TV Logie award and been nominated for a Gold Logie, Australia's top people's choice award. She will take to the road for her first-ever national tour — the 'Visualise Tour' — in July 2005. With the powerful record company, Sony, behind her, Delta is taking on the US market. She owns a luxury Sydney apartment in the same building as Russell Crowe, and is a celebrity in Europe through her TV role in *Neighbours*, her chart success, her ill-fated love match with tennis star Mark Philippoussis and her romance with Brian McFadden.

But those close to her have seen her at her rawest moments throughout this journey to stardom. She has raged against failure, and exulted in the euphoria of success. Delta has felt the power of youth and the fear of death. And she has fallen in love, had her heart broken, and been betrayed.

For Delta, this is just the beginning.

"I was quiet and focused when doing things I wanted to do. But when it came to maths, I was noisy . . . Music is what I wanted to be doing."

Delta

CHAPTER 2

Born to Try

A little girl with oversize glasses stands in front of her mother's video camera. She is shy and giggly. 'I love to sing and dance,' she says. 'And today I'm going to sing one of my favourite songs . . .'

Then Delta takes off her glasses and tosses her hair. She belts out *I Feel the Earth Move*.

It's a fascinating moment. The footage of Delta as a little girl reveals just how early she embraced her destiny. This was no ordinary child singing away. This was a true performer, who knew from an early age that she would be a singer. Delta said later about her vision for her future that 'there wasn't ever a time when I didn't have my eyes tunnel-visioned towards it'.

Fittingly, Delta means 'brightest star in the constellation'. But the dictionary is not where Lea found the name for her first-born child. While pregnant with her daughter, Lea went with her husband, Denis, to a Joe Cocker concert and the gravel-voiced rocker sang *Delta Lady*. The name stayed in Lea's head throughout her pregnancy.

Lea's little Delta Lady was born prematurely on 9 November 1984, at 12.36 am, under the sign of Scorpio — the sign of determination.

Lea jokes about her daughter's birth that 'it was the last time she was early for anything'. Delta describes herself as a 'shocker' and 'scary' in the mornings, but Lea soon realised Delta was not content to lie about and watch cartoons once she'd woken up. 'Delta was quite a driven and serious child! The only time she wasn't enjoying herself was when she wasn't doing anything,' Lea recalls. 'But I didn't know she wanted to do everything!'

Especially sing and play the piano. From the age of two, Delta remembers she wanted to play the family's piano. She says she has been singing since she could talk and can't remember a time when she did not feel the passion for performing. It was a dream to perform that came from her soul, and there was no talk in the Goodrem home of wanting to be famous . . . just a little girl who stunned her parents with her wish to sing.

Her neighbours in the leafy cul-de-sac where the Goodrems lived (in Glenhaven, in Sydney's north-western suburbs) were both charmed and amused by Delta's early ambition. While other neighbourhood kids knocked on the door selling raffle tickets or wanting to play with friends, Delta asked her neighbours to buy a 50-cent ticket to watch her perform at her house. She wore her mother's best clothes for costumes and painted rocks to raise extra cash for accessories. Favourite songs at these concerts, held in her mum's back room, were *If I Could Turn Back Time* (with Delta wearing a 'crazy Cher outfit') and Sinéad O'Connor's *Nothing Compares 2 U*.

'The neighbours didn't seem to mind,' Delta remembers. 'Just my brother didn't like it. He pretended to be out when I sang for them.'

But for Delta the childhood concerts in her mother's clothes were a natural way to express herself. In the title track of her album *Innocent Eyes*, she wrote about remembering being a seven-year-old, and wanting to show her mother she could play the piano.

Her mother watched and listened. Lea recalls that the first time she was struck by Delta's talent was when she performed *Hopelessly Devoted to You* at Lea's father's fortieth birthday karaoke party at the Baulkham Hills Council Chambers. 'Delta sang her heart out,' Lea remembers. 'Everybody said she was amazing.'

'She was incredible,' says family friend, Network Ten news-reader, Ron Wilson. 'From the time she could walk she wanted to perform. She was a precocious and upfront kid, who would sing for us at her parents' dinner parties. She was mesmerising because of her ability to perform without embarrassment at only eight or nine. At first some thought she was showing off but, as the years went on, it became apparent how focused and serious she was about it.'

Yet their daughter's precocious talent took the Goodrems by surprise. 'Denis and I are not musically talented,' Lea insists. 'We were more of a sporting family. Delta was so definite about what she wanted to do and what lessons she wanted, even from a young age. We were in denial at first — we said go and play tennis! But we discovered her commitment was so great that we got behind her. I wasn't sure if it was talent, because I didn't know the difference. But I knew she was really serious. At six and seven, she was a very serious child. She knew what she wanted to do . . . I always thought she was special, that she had something she had to do.'

But Lea also noted Delta's sense of humour and cheeky impersonations, which tempered her seriousness and intensity, and her bright and sunny positive attitude. 'She's a fantastic mimic,' Lea laughs. 'She can mimic any performer and you would think it really is them . . . Cher, Bruce Springsteen . . . anyone you can name. Her favourite? I'm not telling!'

At age ten, Delta told the family what they already knew — she wanted to be a performer. They gave her a microphone for Christmas. 'They thought I was crazy,' Delta confessed once. 'Music had skipped Mum and Dad's generation.'

A defining moment of Delta's ambition was when she met Olivia Newton-John by chance while on a holiday overseas with her family. Delta explained that Olivia came over when she heard their accents and introduced herself. Even at such an early age, Delta, it seemed, attracted stardom where others passed unnoticed.

To satisfy Delta's musical devotion, Lea enrolled her at the Australian College of Entertainment (ACE) at Castle Hill. Every Saturday from 9 am to 6 pm, Lea took Delta to voice, dance and piano lessons. 'She has dedicated herself to Delta's career,' says Ron Wilson.

The college is in a bush setting in Castle Hill, Sydney, close to where Delta grew up. It continues to nurture girls inspired by Delta and its website boasts that she was a former student. Roxanne Kiely, Delta's vivacious singing teacher at the college, remains close to Delta and continued to give her lessons until recently.

A performer in her own right, Roxanne now teaches privately around The Hills district of Sydney and publicises her association with the star on her website. Roxanne is so proud of her link with Delta that she reproduces on her website an interview about her time with Delta that was originally published in the local paper, the *Hills Shire Times*:

'I started teaching Delta when she was only eight years old. I was seeing her once a week, sometimes twice a week for many years. She'd come to lessons and say, "Hi Miss, how are you? You look lovely today." She comes across as such a nice girl. She was like that as an eight year old, and she's like that now.

'At the Australian College of Entertainment, there was always a lot of stress with rehearsals and things. But Delta was always up and happy. Often she'd be waiting for her lesson and while I made myself a cup of coffee, she would be there singing her little songs. It seems like yesterday.'

Roxanne later invited Delta to be part of her Masque Choir Group, which performed at the Jenolan Caves in the Blue Mountains for award-winning documentary maker Greg Grainger, for *The World Around Us* special about the area called *Blue Mountains Magic*. She sang the song *Biomea*, which was based on an Aboriginal legend and Delta performed this solo during the atmospheric concert.

'Delta looked angelic in a white dress,' remembers Greg. 'She looked absolutely stunning — she stood out even then. She was just so attractive and charismatic.' Her voice soared above the choir in the solo. Greg remembers the night as a riveting performance.

Rehearsals for this show were held in Parramatta, in a space above the local McDonald's. Greg remembers that all the girls were well-disciplined and professional. 'They were so dead keen to be filmed. There were no helicopters ferrying them around. They all had to go to the Jenolan Caves with their parents.'

Delta's early promise, creativity, drive and dedication are the hallmarks of many successful artists as children. Beyoncé Knowles, one of Delta's favourite artists and the lead singer of Destiny's Child, was writing songs and winning dance contests at the age of nine. Delta says she began writing her own material at eleven years old and that her first song was called *When Raindrops Fall*.

'When I look back on these songs, I think — I must have been a serious kid,' Delta reflects of her early efforts.

The well-mannered, well-brought-up schoolgirl's enthusiasm for singing is remembered by everyone she came in contact with around her Castle Hill home. 'I did her hair from when she was a little kid, right up until just before she was famous and got the job on *Neighbours*,' says Katrina Mileto, of Radical Hair at the Castle Towers Shopping Centre. 'She was a nice kid like any other and she's exactly like she comes across on TV. She's not changed since becoming famous at all. But she knew what she wanted. She talked a little bit about her career plans every now and then. Her mum talked about it more.'

Delta also began acting professionally at an early age. She and her mother insist acting was always a sidebar to her first love, singing, and they never sought it out. Fame was never the goal either — performing was.

Her first acting gig came to Delta as an offer to audition for an ad via the school, and her mother agreed. It was one of Goodrem's 'Goodness!' moments, a phrase she loves to use when told something surprising.

Delta's first commercial was for American toy company, Galoob Toys, in which she starred with Bec Cartwright, who was later to star in *Home and Away*. The little girls shared an equal passion for singing and acting. 'We both had to have these American accents,' Delta remembers. 'We had some line like, "This is the greatest!" That's how we met. And then we started doing acting, singing and dancing together.'

Delta acted in other ads and then scored a guest role in the 1980s top-rating soap *A Country Practice*, in which she was memorably bitten by a dog on set. But this painful experience didn't put her off acting. She played 'the she-devil from Year 7', Cynthia Broadhurst, in one episode of the family soap *Hey Dad . . .!* in a guest role with Matthew Krok. Cynthia was a 'rich bitch' who was driven to her private school in her limousine.

'Was she on the show?' Gary Reilly, *Hey Dad . . .!*'s executive producer asks. 'Oh, hang on — yes — Cynthia!'

Gary says that Delta was not long enough on the set to make a lasting impression, but she is one of an impressive list of ex-*Hey*

Dad . . . ! actors who showed early promise and went on to become stars, such as Naomi Watts and Belinda Emmett.

'She would only have been on set for about six hours for that scene,' Gary says. 'We looked for child actors who were good-looking, charming, disciplined, mature and showed talent — so Delta would have had all those qualities. They had to learn their lines and be focused on set. The kids were put into a really adult environment, it was very demanding, so we had to make sure the kids we chose were up to it.'

Delta continued to act until she had to wear braces, and the self-conscious teenager then decided she'd had enough and concentrated instead on school and singing.

Lea and Denis Goodrem wanted the best for their children, so Delta was sent to The Hills Grammar School in Kenthurst. The school, funded by parents who mortgaged their own homes to create it, prides itself on excellence, and Delta delivered that and more. 'She thrived at Hills Grammar,' says Ron Wilson.

Her report cards described a girl with a 'vivid imagination'. Outwardly confident and successful, Delta says at school she was a shy and nervous person who was a sook. Remembering her first day at school, Delta recalls, 'I cried and cried starting school. I didn't want to go. But when people started to talk to me, it was fine.'

'I had a really close group of friends. I was quiet and focused when doing things I wanted to do. But when it came to maths, I was noisy. I was probably always in trouble for not doing my schoolwork, I spent a lot of time facing the wall. It was like, "Goodrem! Out!" Music is what I wanted to be doing.'

While *McLeod's Daughters* and *Hating Alison Ashley* star Rachael Carpani became a friend, as did drama buddy Bec Cartwright,

Delta says that she was 'more friends with guys'. Ron Wilson fondly remembers that Delta was part of a clique at school called the 'pretty people'. 'There were eleven girls out of twenty-eight in her class,' he said. 'So they were prone to cliques.'

Childhood pictures of Delta show her to be chocolate-box pretty. As a toddler, her long little fingers had reached out to touch the keys of the piano; in another photo, she sat by a window, her blonde curls framing a thoughtful face. But in later school photos, Delta's hair was already growing long and had darkened to its natural brown. Her smile was beautiful, confident and happy. Delta says she has always regarded her smile as 'part of her'.

Katrina Mileto, Delta's childhood hairdresser at Radical Hair, remembers Delta always looked beautiful and well groomed. 'Her hairstyle was always the same — the long hair. It was easy to maintain. Sometimes she came in every week, sometimes twice a week, sometimes not for a few weeks. She wasn't doing any gigs though at that stage. She never tried to dye her own hair at home and make a mess of it or anything like that.'

But those who know Delta say she was never vain. 'She has no idea how good-looking she is,' a friend says fondly. For Delta, her aim to please was not through her looks — it was through her singing and personality. Wanting to be everybody's friend, Delta says that she didn't know if she was 'cool or not . . . I was just cruising along'.

In fact, she was everybody's friend, became school captain and made a point of talking to the little kids. She hated bitching or gossiping, saying she preferred guys because it was more straightforward. 'They just bash each other up, you know?' From an early age, Delta stuck to her view, 'If you can't say anything nice, don't say anything at all!'

As a schoolgirl and aspiring star, Delta had five male friends whom she describes as her best mates. 'They were so loyal to me.' She says that boys were never really on her agenda romantically, but she did have a teenage romance with Jay Till, whom she met at a party. When casting his mind back over that time, Ron Wilson says that Delta was always drawn to sportspeople, and AFL Sydney Swans star Jude Bolton sprang to mind when asked about Delta and boyfriends. But Delta has always said that while he remains one of her closest friends and supporters, the relationship has always been platonic.

Her second-hand uniforms and textbooks signed with her name are now hotly contested items among the students of Hills Grammar, while her voice and her energy is what other students and parents most remember about her. 'She was always one of those kids who got up and sang,' says Ron Wilson, whose son James attended school with Delta. 'From a young age, she was always performing in something or other. You knew she'd go places. She had so much energy — she still does.'

The Wilson family went to Hamilton Island with the Goodrems, and to the Gold Coast. 'I remember Delta was rehearsing lines by the pool for a commercial,' says Ron of that holiday. 'The rest of us were lying around. But she wasn't forced. She wanted to do it.'

'She was so focused on a being a singer,' reflects Joanne Meehan, a family friend and NSW state manager of the Look Good . . . Feel Better program, which assists women undergoing treatment for cancer by providing free skincare and beauty advice. 'I remember she sang when she was fourteen at a local fundraiser for us. I was blown away. She sang a Mariah Carey song I think . . . and I remember watching her and this amazing voice came out of the little girl who was so beautiful.'

'Delta was always into singing rather than an acting career,' says Katrina Mileto. 'So far as I can remember, from the age of about fifteen that was all she talked about. She was always happy. She didn't really talk about having a master plan of how to make it come true — she just wanted to get an album done. I just knew she always wanted to be a singer, but we didn't talk about it a lot. Delta used to talk about all the things other teenagers would talk about — school and friends and that sort of thing.'

She sang with Rolf Harris at a school concert, her hair neatly pushed back with a red ribbon and her Hills Grammar T-shirt tucked into her jeans. This early clip is included in her DVD, *Delta*. 'We had so much fun putting that video together,' says Lea fondly. 'I think it shows Delta's sense of humour.'

'Delta, where's Delta?' Harris calls out on the video. 'Oh! There you are!' Delta emerges from the crowd, gives one of her trademark smiles, and steps up to the microphone. The DVD also includes the *Hey Dad . . . !* clip of her playing Cynthia, her ads and a cute spoof of Delta holding her brother, Trent, while she plays the role of Superwoman.

Hills Grammar's Community Relations Director, Elisabeth Pellinkhof, says the school is incredibly proud of their student's success. 'Delta loves performing and the school has been happy to accommodate her on her wonderful journey,' she says.

Delta performed in the school play, *The Lion, the Witch and the Wardrobe*, and joined the school's Gifted and Talented program.

She participated in the Tournament of the Minds, in which she focused on problem-solving through creativity and performance.

While gifted children often struggle with friendships, Delta managed to maintain her popularity. But, as she later wrote in her song *Innocent Eyes*, her singing ambitions also attracted teasing, something she attributes to taking the chance to dream of stardom when she was only fifteen.

'I had so many troubles at school,' Delta said once. 'You're always going to be knocked by people, but you have to hang in there.'

Ron Wilson says Delta's amazing determination to be a singer brought its share of attention at school. 'Look, school is a harsh place. And if you see someone achieving some success and so focused, then there is a lot of jealousy . . . The others think, How can you do it and I can't? The young mind can exaggerate.'

The only other thing Delta gave energy to was sport, and she remains an avid sports watcher, especially AFL because of her love for the Sydney Swans, for whom her brother Trent hopes to play one day. It was the one thing apart from singing that she was passionate about. Lea, ever present in her children's lives and in helping them to achieve their dreams, took Delta to sport activities nearly every afternoon after school.

Delta was in demand on the basketball court, although she says she was always getting injured. She swam competitively and her love of sport encouraged her clean living. 'At school I was silly, then there was the naughty side,' Delta remembers. 'But there was a cut-off point where I was like, "No, guys, I'm not doing that." There's naughty — and there's fun. I'm boring. I don't do cigarettes or drugs. I think it's the sport thing . . . I'm not that interested.'

Delta moves to Melbourne, 2002

Delta with Sydney Swans player Jude Bolton, 2001

"I'm boring. I don't do cigarettes or drugs. I think it's the sport thing . . . I'm not that interested."

Delta

A friend recalls that Delta's clean living is the real deal. From an early age, Delta made it clear she wasn't keen on experimenting like her peers. 'She's never had a drug in her life,' he says. 'She doesn't smoke and she hardly drinks.'

Because of the trust that the Goodrems placed in their young daughter, Delta was never given a curfew when she went out. They had an understanding that she would be home early. It was part of what she said was her natural inclination to stick by the rules, knowing her parents were behind whatever she chose to do.

An avid skier, the elegant teen was as focused on achieving in sport as she was in her music, and passionately pursued skiing during family holidays to the snow in Australia and abroad. Revealing her extraordinary ambition, Delta says seriously, 'At fourteen, I came second in the slalom race of the NSW interschool competition. It was a big decision whether to go to Canada and start racing seriously, or do my demo CD. But as much as I love skiing, music is my passion. I had to choose between singing or going to Canada to train professionally.'

From this early age, whether it was on skis or on the stage, it had to be straight for the top. Otherwise, what was the point?

The Goodrems taught their children the value of hard work, and Delta now passes these values on to her fans. Delta often talks in clichés but she truly believes in these sentiments: If it's worth doing, it's worth doing well. If you can't say anything nice, don't say anything at all — at least in public. And life is not a dress rehearsal.

Her brother follows the mantra too. Delta is close to Trent and is proud that he is as focused on achieving his dream to be a professional AFL player as she is about singing. Delta says they are a high-achieving and competitive family. As young teenagers, Trent and his older sister made a pact that one day she would perform at a grand final match he was playing in.

While extremely close, the siblings competed over almost everything. 'My brother and I would always have whistling contests and we'd end up in tears, fighting over which one of us was the better whistler!' Delta remembers. The family is so competitive and spirited they have a trophy competition. Delta's now includes her seven ARIAs and a Silver Logie next to her basketball and skiing awards.

While Delta eventually chose singing, she couldn't help striving to win everything else too. She and her brother were both up for a coveted award at school: the Sportsperson of the Year. Delta was in Year 10, and Trent in Year 8. Her drive to perform on the sports field was another way she revealed her ambition. Her friendly 'cruising' personality at school masked a fierce drive, nervous energy and a cool head that never lost sight of the future.

During the rare moments when she was sprawled on the couch, Delta would watch her 'all-time favourite movie', *Grease*, and sing along to *Hopelessly Devoted to You*. 'The first time I heard her sing *Hopelessly Devoted to You*, I had my mouth open,' says a childhood friend. Delta loved the fact that Olivia was 'classy', that she sang and acted and toured the world.

She dreamed that soon it would be her. She'd be just like Olivia. A classy, international star.

"She has an 'It' factor. There's something about her that lights up a room. When she sings, she takes your breath away. She has the spirit and the challenge."

Glenn Wheatley

CHAPTER 3

Believe in Me

In a fashionable Sydney hotel on Sydney's Oxford Strip, the Burdekin, Sony executives gathered at the bar and then made their way to a reserved room. A sense of jaded curiosity hung in the air as they waited for the promised talent to showcase her stuff. They had been in this situation a hundred times before.

But Glenn Wheatley and Lea Goodrem knew it was the most important night of Delta's life. The teenage singer had been rehearsing every night for a month to showcase to Sony executives. She was excited, nervous and scared.

It was just before the opening of the 2000 Sydney Olympics, and the atmosphere was ripe for fairytales. During this heady month, a prince would fall in love with an Australian girl in a pub, and Cathy Freeman and Ian Thorpe would realise their dreams to earn the adoration of Australia. Standing on the cusp of her future, Delta was just as determined as these Olympic athletes to perform. But Australia was yet to listen.

Glenn Wheatley had organised the night with one goal in mind: to get Sony Music to sign Delta Goodrem. He'd picked the Burdekin Hotel because it was close to Sony Music's headquarters in East Sydney.

Record label BMG had already knocked the beautiful teenager back after hearing her demo. Glenn had also presented to Roadshow Music, but no deal with them had eventuated. Now Glenn believed that if the head of Sony Music, Denis Handlin, saw Delta live, it might be a different story. 'She has an "It" factor. There's something about her that lights up a room. When she sings, she takes your breath away. She has the spirit and the challenge,' Wheatley said once of his confidence in Delta.

As John Farnham's agent, Wheatley could gain a powerful

audience when he needed to. And he was convinced Delta deserved to be heard. 'He was blown away by her,' says a friend. 'Absolutely thought she was an amazing talent.'

Delta had first come to Wheatley's attention via a red-and-white striped envelope. The Sydney Swans supporter and part-owner of the team couldn't resist opening the package in his favourite team's colours. It was just the reaction fourteen-year-old Delta wanted when she sent her demo to the Sydney Swans Club, hoping it would be passed on to Wheatley.

'I really wanted a gig doing the national anthem somewhere. Being a Sydney Swans fan, I really wanted to do it at one of their games. Then a friend of a friend said Glenn Wheatley was involved with the Sydney Swans. So I sent him my demo. Glenn said he was walking past and saw this red-and-white thingy and was thinking, Good, it's not music — he loves the Swans — and he picked it up, opened it and went, "Ahh!" and then he listened to it and then he called me,' Delta recalled in early interviews.

Her determination to get to Wheatley — one of the highest profile managers in Australia — is an insight into Delta's focus on achieving her dreams. A friend of the family describes her as an 'old soul' who never doubted her own destiny. She also realised from an early age that money would give her the tools to achieve her dreams.

'All the money I saved from acting, I put in the bank,' Delta recalls. 'Mum and Dad said to me, "Hold onto that money until you are older and you can put it towards a car, or you can put it towards something else as an investment." I said, "This is what I want to do. I want to make a demo." So when I was thirteen, I used my savings and recorded five songs I had written.'

The demo was recorded at a studio in Crows Nest, Sydney, with Delta's piano teacher, Michael Kieran Harvey, who is one of Australia's most respected classical pianists. Never one to do things by halves, fourteen-year-old Delta ordered 200 copies.

'She was writing songs though, and she brought her CDs in a few times for us to listen to,' remembers Katrina Mileto. 'They were home-made demo CDs she had done in a studio. She was very proud of them. She did it a few times — two or three — just before she got the *Neighbours* job. But I don't remember ever hearing the tracks again. I don't think they were ones that have gone on to be famous. They were the same kind of piano ballads that she's famous for now though. She played them to everyone in the salon on the stereo system. Everyone was impressed with how good it sounded, but not surprised. I knew she could sing, but it did sound better with all the production that goes into a professional CD. I knew she could sing because she used to sing while I was doing her hair. While she was sitting in the hairdresser's chair, she would practise her scales, singing notes and doing singing exercises.'

'I sent the demo to people, along with photos of myself and a résumé,' Delta explains. 'I wasn't sure who to send it to. I just sent it out to lots of people, I sent it to my friends and my parents' friends.' She sent it to Sony, who politely rejected the demo but said encouragingly she had talent that needed further developing.

Then it came to Wheatley: a little red-and-white package of fate. As a manager he is routinely sent so many demos he says that if he listened to them all he wouldn't have a life. But in this case, he was intrigued enough to listen and arrange a meeting. 'I saw confidence, and the spark of ingenuity,' he said in interviews about his time with Delta.

'She knew I was a former director, part-owner and passionate supporter of the Swans, and I thought, That's smart. Then I put the CD on and was blown away. I thought, This girl can sing. From the photo she sent with it, I knew she was good-looking too. But one of the most important things was she was so genuinely enthusiastic and determined.'

Wheatley heard Delta's demo and initially thought she had potential but was too young to develop properly. He hadn't counted on Delta's determination, or the supportive force of her mother. Delta had wanted this since she was five, so 'no' was not an option. 'Right from the start, I knew there was a plan in place,' Wheatley later said about Delta.

When Wheatley phoned he spoke to both Lea and Delta, and Lea's mother agreed to a meeting with him at the Observatory Hotel in Sydney. It was November 1998 and Delta still wore braces.

Wheatley has said that Delta was exceptional for her age, and so anxious to get going, with strong family support. Although continuing to fear that she was too young, he recognised her enormous potential and decided to sign her to his management company, TalentWorks.

'Wheatley was always confident about her talent and she was going to be one of his biggest acts ever,' says a friend. 'He knew he was on to a winner, but he didn't realise how long it would take to get there. He was absolutely blown away by her talent and potential, but wanted to wait until she was older before approaching record companies.'

She spent the next eighteen months juggling school, writing more material and going to Melbourne. As she became close to Wheatley, she also spent time with his son, Tim. He became a

"At fifteen, **Delta** was **ready**. So was **Vanessa Amorosi**. Not every kid is like them. You have to be ready for it, to be mature. Delta has **greatness in her heart**."

Mark Holden

member of her band and is now signed to his father's management company as an artist.

'Tim gave Delta her first kiss,' says a friend. 'They had a brief teenage romance. She was only fifteen and I think he was about seventeen. She adored him, but they quickly realised it was not a good idea as he was her manager's son.' In what would become her trademark, Delta wrote a love song about Tim that would be included in her first — and unlikely ever to be released — CD. She also performed in a film clip, which she would later claim was amateurish and unflattering.

Those who met Delta at this time were struck by her warm personality, but they also sensed the complexity and strength of character underneath the genuine beauty and sweetness. Says a source who knew her at the time, 'You could tell she definitely knew what she wanted and she wasn't prepared to compromise.'

'She was such a sweet, gorgeous and naive girl,' adds a friend. 'The thing that really struck me was that she had this amazing powerful voice and confidence, and so tall and pretty, but when you spoke to her at length it was like speaking to a child because she was so, so innocent, sweet and sheltered. She was like a little girl.'

Wheatley arranged for Delta to spend time with two Melbourne producers, Paul Higgins and Trevor Carter of Empire Records, to develop Delta's potential. Recalling their time with the young star in an interview with the *Herald Sun*, Higgins says he and business partner Carter became close to Delta. 'She was like a member of the family. We came to know her well. She spent so many hundreds of hours here at a time, virtually living in our pockets.'

The pair took the fourteen-year-old to her first ARIAs in 1999, where she was mistaken for Britney Spears on the red carpet. 'She thought that was cool,' he remembers. The star gave a 'sincere smile and a firm handshake' to everyone she met.

They recalled that in the studio Delta was a clumsy kid who spilt the coffee. 'She is a complete klutz,' says a friend affectionately. 'She's all legs — this tall, gorgeous, gangly teenager who trips over her shoelaces and walks into walls. She's a dag — and I mean that in the most affectionate way — who has absolutely no idea of how good-looking she is.'

But Higgins says he was most struck by this gawky, innocent teenager's cool ambition and determination. They recorded Delta's first demo, a twelve-track CD simply called *Delta*, which they claim helped clinch the deal with Sony Music. They now feel that their role in helping the star is often overlooked and nobody believes they were part of Delta's early career until they show them the photos. 'Some people doubt it happened. That's when I pull out the photos and say, "Here, it did happen. We did work with her."'

Higgins and Carter later commenced legal action (now resolved) to try to release that first album, *Delta*, to a record company against the wishes of the Goodrem family. But sources close to the family say Delta never forgot their role in her career, and point out that she has remained friends with many of those who helped in the early days, such as Roxanne Kiely, her first singing teacher.

'I think we helped determine her future to become a singer and an artist,' Higgins said once. 'She had all the ability and talent. It was just a matter of focus . . . There is hardly anything she can't do.'

Especially given the chance to sing in front of the most powerful man in the Australian music industry, Denis Handlin, that night at the Burdekin.

'I got my four dancers and backing track ready to showcase,' Delta recalled of the night. 'I was so determined and we rehearsed every night for a month. I was nervous, but I had nothing to lose. I'd practised so much that my singing and dancing were fantastic.'

Her hard work paid off. That night Sony Music's CEO did something extremely rare: he signed her on the spot. He signalled Wheatley mid-performance and said, 'I want to talk business.'

In an interview about the star with leading music journalist Christine Sams, Handlin said, 'She just blew me away completely. For a start I was just so impressed by what a stunning-looking kid she was. But she sounded as fantastic as she looked. She was very nervous on that day and she had a few dancers with her. She worked really hard on getting the routines right — I heard she had been working on it a few weeks. She's a perfectionist.' Handlin added that, most of all, Delta is a 'decent kid; D is for decent'.

When Delta was told the news, she was beside herself with excitement. She recalls, 'Glenn said, "Congratulations, you are a Sony girl." There was all this screaming and hugging. It was one of the most exciting moments of my life. I'd worked so hard for it — all those weekends and nights dancing and singing.' At fifteen, and without any profile, Delta had pulled off a recording deal with one of the biggest music companies in the world.

That night she celebrated at home with some girlfriends. Her then boyfriend, Jay Till, later told journalist Frank Thorne that he snuck out of his parents' house to be with her when she insisted he come over and celebrate. She and her girlfriends danced around the house and Delta had a glass of champagne. 'She is so, so clean,' says a friend.

In the beginning Delta was a Sony girl who nobody noticed. She was lost in the giant record company's priority list. These days the Sony Sydney office is plastered with posters of Delta.

But if Sony wasn't really paying attention in those early days, Delta was. She was determined to make an impression. Wheatley organised a suitably glamorous first live performance for her at the opening of Tiffany's new store in Melbourne, where he was based. The teenager sang *Diamonds Are Forever* and *Moon River*, because of the connection with the film *Breakfast at Tiffany's*.

She soaked up her exciting new surroundings and treated glamorous industry events as seriously as a college lecture in the entertainment world. At the ARIAs she sat quietly with Wheatley on a Sony table, absorbing the atmosphere around her.

'People wouldn't have known I was there — but I was . . . watching how other celebrities and other people act,' she said of this time.

She noted in her journal how some celebrities treated their fans badly and vowed that when she was famous too, she would be far more respectful and grateful. As the excited teens reached out to others, Delta was already planning the moment when one day they would cry out her name.

Former pop star and *Australian Idol* judge, Mark Holden, was working as a consultant with Sony at this time, helping them nurture new talent. While poring over some half-forgotten demos in the Sony office, he came across the demo Delta had made with Higgins.

He told *Woman's Day* he went to Handlin and urged him to make Delta a priority. 'She was at Sony without anyone putting any focus on her. Essentially, I became her champion.' He worked with the young singer for the next two years on what he called 'Project Delta'.

'There was a long period of time where it was really difficult to get people behind her,' Mark said of his time with the star. 'She was fifteen then — but even at that age, whenever there was a problem she'd come back with a solution. She made a video with a photographer friend off her own bat. She designed another video herself where she budgeted, flat-planned and put a whole presentation together. At that age, it was wildly impressive stuff. Whenever she hits a wall, she finds ways to get over it.'

Today, as Mark judges a new batch of sixteen-year-old aspiring Deltas in the *Idol* competition, he still recalls her poise, ambition and maturity. In an interview with *New Idea* about *Idol*, Mark said, 'At fifteen, Delta was ready. So was Vanessa Amorosi. Not every kid is like them. You have to be ready for it, to be mature. Delta has greatness in her heart.'

Delta and Mark Holden began co-writing songs. Delta again went with the flow and said at the time that it was 'all good', but she later admitted that many of the songs they wrote in those early days together were never really true to her, although three were ultimately included in her album.

One of those early songs, *Let's Dance* (penned by Mark Holden, Delta and Axel Breitung), has recently been released by tween queen Nikki Webster, and another song, *Blush*, to Delta's amusement later became a hit in Denmark. 'We travelled to Germany together and did a lot of these great up-tempo songs,' Delta says. 'But other bands are singing them now. I've no doubt some will do well, but they weren't for me.'

While Delta now has the chart success to prove she knows best, at this time she was much more malleable and suppressed her gnawing feeling that standard 'Britney-pop' wasn't her destiny. But when Wheatley went to songwriter Steve Kipner and asked him for a song for Delta, she and Sony agreed on the pop tune, *I Don't Care*. She was encouraged by the fact that Steve Kipner had worked with John Farnham, written for Olivia Newton-John and penned Christina Aguilera's massive hit, *Genie in a Bottle*.

In the film clip that accompanied the single's release, directed by Anthony Rose, Delta desperately tries to be a young pop starlet. She tosses her hair and runs away with a smouldering male model, Oscar, who looks like her future boyfriend Mark Philippoussis's younger brother.

She looks embarrassed in the love scenes and self-conscious in a midriff top in a wheat field. The song is catchy — but forgettable. In retrospect, the song and video were so at odds with Delta's true nature that they failed to ring true.

But while she does look uncomfortable, Anthony Rose says Delta had a lot of input into the video and, true to form, knew what she wanted from the outset. 'She was very serious and passionate from a young age. She was never a giggly little girl. She was very professional and very rehearsed, more so than most. I thought she was a great singer,' Anthony remembers.

'She and her mother had a very strong idea of what they wanted. She didn't wear anything she didn't want to wear. She wanted a video that was a little sexy . . . but not too sexy. She didn't want a video that threw herself out there. She wanted a romantic Romeo-and-Juliet feel. I think she was experimenting. When I met her, they were formative years.'

A journalist who met Delta during these early days remembers a beautiful girl in clothes that didn't seem right for her. 'She seemed to be trying to be older. She had low-slung jeans, stilettos and heavy make-up on.'

'She was so gorgeous, she had no idea how pretty she was,' says a friend. 'She looked beautiful and young just in jeans and T-shirts, but would always be dressed in these frilly clothes. The stylists clashed with Delta and Lea in the beginning.

'Lea and Delta didn't like the younger, funkier outfits that the stylists wanted her to wear and Lea would not budge on anything. A number of stylists were very frustrated and said the Goodrems had to be more flexible. There was concern about her looking too sexy, but look — nobody was trying to get her into bikinis. Eventually Sony stepped in and a tacit compromise was reached.'

She was young and yet to develop her own style of fashion, just as she was struggling to find her musical heart. Delta desperately wanted to please her record company. She once remarked 'I get really upset if I can't hear my gut instinct. I'm a big instinct follower.'

In *I Don't Care*, Delta wears a midriff top and jeans, her hair is straight and her make-up funky. It's a conventional pop look which helped lose Delta among the crowd of wannabe pop artists, just like the song. It was barely indistinguishable from the reams of other young pretty stars with a pop tune.

Delta insisted she was happy with the track. Echoing Anthony Rose, she enthusiastically said it was a Romeo-and-Juliet song and that it had her signature on it. 'I'm really looking forward to this being a long career because I love it so much,' she said at the time. 'I have to believe in and visualise it. I hope it works.'

But the song was a failure. Delta wanted No. 1 and the best *I Don't Care* did was No. 64. 'I was surprised when the video did not do as well as we hoped,' Anthony reflects today.

In her bedroom, surrounded by her teddy-bear and fairy collection, Delta had put the ARIA chart on her wall. She had white-outed the current No. 1 single and written instead '*I Don't Care*'. To Delta, there had never been any question it would be a huge hit. As she stared at the poster on her wall where her No. 1 single was scratched in over another hit, she felt overwhelmed with disappointment, shock and anger. She had never failed at anything before. Yet here was the most important thing she had ever done — release a single — fading fast off the Top 100.

The song title couldn't have been more ironic. Delta cared so much she thought she was going to explode. 'I am so passionate about my music,' she said. 'The highs are so high and the lows are so low.'

Her friends were perplexed by the song choice. 'My friends said, "Why aren't you doing a song that makes people cry?"' Delta said later about *I Don't Care*. 'I said, "Because it's hip." But they didn't believe me, standing there with a mean face.'

Delta put on a brave front, but she was shattered. She was forced to sit on the sidelines as her career stalled, while other singers connected with the public. Delta is a spirited and generous person, but even she found it hard to swallow as she later sat back and watched her friend Bec Cartwright's success and saw her singing plans take off on the back of her popular *Home and Away* profile. Likewise, *Neighbours* starlet Holly Valance released *Kiss Kiss* and had a No. 1 hit with it in the UK.

As she struggled to find a new direction, her ambition blocked

"I get really upset if I can't hear my **gut instinct**. I'm a **big instinct** follower."

Delta

by an uninterested public, Delta became more and more frustrated. 'She would ring me and ask, "Why has Holly Valance got a song in the charts? Why has Rebecca got a song?"' Wheatley claimed in an interview with leading music journalist, the *Sun Herald*'s Christine Sams. 'I told her to forget all that, and look ahead.'

'She was so disappointed because her expectations were so high,' says a friend sympathetically. 'Her whole life had been geared towards that moment, and she'd failed. I think she probably thought that if the single failed her career was over. She compared herself endlessly to others doing well in the charts and really struggled to understand why they had success and she didn't. She wanted everything yesterday and she wanted it so, so badly.'

Delta admitted she was angry about the flop. Desperately and relentlessly she tried to find the positive. 'After *I Don't Care*, I had to take a step back and look at what happened and build myself back up. It wasn't even something I wanted to do but you learn.'

Delta said of the bitter experience, 'I still love that song. I'm not going to look at it as a flop. If I hadn't released that song, *Neighbours* wouldn't have asked me to join their show.'

For Sony, it was a lesson learned too. They'd pushed Delta onto the market without considering her individuality and unique talents. For a girl who doesn't think she is sexy and who is embarrassed by nakedness, trying to be an overtly sexy pop star was destined to fall flat. 'Sexy girls are the ones with the cool pout,' Delta says. 'I smile too much.'

While her official Sony bio boasts, 'This is no manufactured pop star', in the beginning that is what she was. 'It was Britney — crap, really,' says a friend. 'In a way she was trying to be presented as more sexy and mature than she was. She never wanted to be sexy or Britney. She is gorgeous, but sex appeal is for other girls.'

Her friends urged her to go back to the Delta they knew, the girl who wrote songs that made them cry. But the person who most felt she needed to follow her heart and instinct was Delta herself, and it was Delta who eventually found the uniqueness that would stun Australia.

'To think she believed she had failed, that her career was over, and not to know the incredible success around the corner,' reflects a friend.

To Sony's credit, and Delta's enormous relief, they went back to the drawing board and allowed Delta to create her own identity and complete her album, *Innocent Eyes*. Michael Taylor, head of Artist and Repertoire at Sony Music, was concerned that ballads usually didn't do well on radio, but he was so impressed with her song writing and piano that he thought it was worth the risk, as did Denis Handlin.

'Denis loves a ballad,' says a music insider, unsurprised Handlin warmed so much to his young singer. He, like Delta, knew it was her true path as an artist, and Taylor put her in touch with other writers to help fine-tune her raw material.

'After that we sat down and listened,' Handlin admitted to Christine Sams. 'She was this young girl, but she was passionate. She kept saying, "Oh please, I write my own songs. I don't want to be cast as someone's look-alike . . . I want to be myself."'

For Delta, Sony's agreement was music to her ears. As she later wrote in *Born To Try*, it was time to do what she truly believed.

"She's the most beautiful person I've ever met. She's got a **heart of gold** and a **mind like a diamond.**"

Blair McDonough

CHAPTER 4

Everybody Needs Neighbours

On a crisp autumn morning in Melbourne, the girl who loves to sleep in woke for her first day on the set of *Neighbours*. As the slumber lifted, Delta considered the day ahead with her characteristic nervous excitement.

According to a friend, the most exciting thing of all about the *Neighbours* offer for Delta had everything to do with being a love-struck teenager. As she dressed for her first day on set as Nina Tucker, a young man's face floated into her mind.

'You know why she was excited to get the *Neighbours* part? It meant she would get to meet Blair. She was in love with him!'

Blair McDonough had come to prominence in 2001 in a bizarre and thoroughly modern way — via the first season of reality TV show *Big Brother*. He had done nothing more than live in a house that was seen by millions of people, and have them like him enough to keep him in the house until the last night with Ben Williams.

Her teenage crush on Blair aside, there was no doubt that *Neighbours* was a massive opportunity for her. She hadn't expected this turn of events. But always one to seize a chance, she wasn't about to say no to restarting her acting career and it was an exciting boost on top of the encouraging new start to her music. 'It was a whole new chapter for me,' Delta said. 'A real catalyst to moving on.'

Since the bitter disappointment of *I Don't Care*, Delta had been focusing on her debut album. She was fine-tuning her piano-based ballads and original songs with a series of industry songwriters who Michael Taylor thought would suit the young singer's new direction.

With the support of her parents, she reluctantly left school to

Delta as Nina, 2003

Delta with Blair at the 2002 Bastille Day Ball

concentrate on her dream. 'She loved school and did well, but singing was always her priority,' says a friend.

In the midst of this new start, Delta screen-tested for *Neighbours*. Although still on air, starlet Holly Valance had just left to continue her pop career, and the TV show had already successfully launched singers Natalie Imbruglia and one of Delta's role models, Kylie Minogue. The show decided to turn the tables and introduce a singer who already had a record deal and a character that wanted to be a singer into the show.

While it has been suggested that Glenn Wheatley was responsible for taking Delta to *Neighbours,* with the hope of following the success of Kylie Minogue, a former Network Ten executive confirms that *Neighbours* did indeed find Delta, and the idea to write a singer into the show blossomed when they discovered her.

'*Neighbours* former chief executive producer, Stanley Walsh, discovered Delta and brought a tape in to the network,' says the former Ten executive. 'Delta was obviously a brilliant singer with a great future. She also did an impressive screen test proving she was a terrific find for the program. It was logical to create a character which incorporated that potential.'

Stanley Walsh regards Delta as one of his great finds, but says he literally came across her by chance. 'We needed to find a new girl after Holly Valance left. I saw an article about Delta in the *Herald Sun*. And I thought she was gorgeous, she had acting experience from *Hey Dad* and was sixteen, so just the right age. We are always looking for new talent because the stars — well, they grow up. Kym Valentine is in her twenties now and a mum.

'We weren't necessarily looking for a singer, but it was an added bonus. I rang Glenn Wheatley and arranged a meeting with him and Delta. When I met her, I thought, What a knockout. She was so sweet, and so fresh and open. I arranged an audition — and look, she was inexperienced, but the thing that came across was what a beautiful person she was. We had a drama coach on *Neighbours* and anything that involves five days a week, well, you're inevitably going to get better.'

Jan Russ, casting director at *Neighbours* for twenty years, is regarded as a 'star maker' whose eye for talent discovered Kylie Minogue, Natalie Imbruglia, Guy Pearce, Holly Valance and Russell Crowe. She was also impressed with her colleague's find. When asked how Delta compared to Kylie, Jan says, 'Delta had a different magic — she is a different flower.'

Delta was not the only singer considered for *Neighbours*. 'Until they saw Delta, producers had wanted Chloe Lattanzi,' claims a source. Lattanzi is the daughter of Delta's idol, Olivia Newton-John. But former Network Ten drama executive, Rick Maier, says that isn't strictly true. 'The production company, Grundy Television, presents new talent to the network for consideration,' he explains. 'From memory, both girls did screen tests, but not at the same time. They weren't competing for the same role. A role was specifically created for Delta.'

When they found Delta, they realised she was exactly what they wanted — young, unknown, talented, and contracted to a record company. In short, a singer on the verge of stardom. Says Ben Michaels, who crafted the character of Nina, 'It was fun to think we had this raw talent that no one knew about . . . yet!'

Delta knew it was a gift of an opportunity. Kylie was a role model, and she'd learnt from bitter experience how Holly had enjoyed success on the charts on the back of her *Neighbours* role, while her own song had flopped. 'It's still very hard to get your music out there,' Delta said. 'So when *Neighbours* approached me to do some music on the show, I said I'd love to.'

Wheatley was excited too. 'We didn't want the soap-star-turned-singer vibe,' he says of the offer. 'But how cool would it be if she was already a singer?'

Delta was concerned she'd be compared to former *Neighbours* pop starlets, then decided she shouldn't worry because she was a singer. She was reassured too by the fact that she was starting to be noticed in the music industry, and her confidence was being rebuilt as she followed her own heart. She had experimented with a whole range of styles, but kept coming back to the powerful ballads that are now her trademark.

Her instinct told her to embrace the *Neighbours* role. 'She liked that she had the credibility of already being signed,' says a friend. 'She was so excited about *Neighbours* and saw it as a huge stepping stone.'

'I was lucky because a lot of people in the industry knew of my music beforehand and kept it separate from my acting,' Delta observes gratefully. She was already trying to prove herself in the music world and nobody, bar some elitists, would deny her the chance to build a profile to help her sales. Apart from *Australian Idol*, *Neighbours* was the best way to get a singer noticed via the mass market, and with its long-running success in the UK, a tried and true way to establish a profile there.

'It's a massive launch pad,' says a music insider bluntly of the show's selling power. '*Neighbours* has a huge and broad audience. But there have been singers from *Neighbours* whose songs were terrible. You have to have a great product.'

Delta later said, with a subtle reference to those actors-turned-singers before her, that she was not using *Neighbours* as a stopping-off point. She described it instead as a 'collaboration of hard work'.

Acting agent Mark Morrissey drafted Delta's contract with the soap as Wheatley had only music experience. The two men had met on the forgettable talent show *Star Search*, and remembering the gentle, respected agent, Wheatley brought in Morrissey's agency to look after Delta's acting interests.

However, according to Wheatley, Delta felt the character wasn't right. The scriptwriters had dreamed up Nina Tucker as being loud and with a mean streak. This concerned Delta. As an actress, as well as a singer-songwriter, she knew acting called for her to play characters far removed from her own. (She had, after all, already played a petulant spoilt rich bitch in the playground on *Hey Dad . . . !*) But Nina would be a character that would spill into her own life when her music was released into the real world. This was her life.

Amazingly — even though she was still an unknown — Delta stuck to her gut instinct and asked for the chance to have some input in creating the role. 'We had a problem with the first character because it was too feisty for Delta,' Wheatley told *TV Hits*. 'She let them know in no uncertain terms that it wasn't her, and she couldn't play it.'

To those who know Delta, her strong views on how Nina's character should be shaped is no surprise and hints at the complexities beneath her perpetually sunny image, which has earned her the nickname 'Saint Delta' among journalists. Delta herself warned, 'I'm a lot more assertive than people think.'

With the role of Nina being created for Delta, she was

fortunate the producers were prepared to mould a character that suited her, rather than the other way around. 'She discussed the role with us and she said she wanted Nina to be a nice, wholesome girl with good morals,' Stanley Walsh confirms. 'She said she did not want her character to be promiscuous, and if she had concerns about her character she would tell us. She said she wanted to be a role model.'

'We reworked the character overnight, before the first scene was shot,' Wheatley explained to *TV Hits*. 'We really worked it, developing the new character of Nina — we saw the timid, shy little girl change over a period of time to a girl with more confidence, who was able to go on and do things like sing in front of an audience. This essentially came from input from Delta.'

Describing her, Delta tellingly says, 'Nina is a quiet, unassuming girl who doesn't think anything of her amazing gifts. She is fun to play, but nothing like me in real life. I have more confidence in my ability, although I too can be very shy.'

Script producer Ben Michaels agrees that Delta is different from her on-screen persona. 'She is a lot more driven than Nina,' he observes.

The opportunity came at personal cost. Unlike *Home and Away*, which is based in Palm Beach, Sydney, *Neighbours* is filmed in Nunawading, Melbourne. The close-knit family had to be split up so Delta could move to Melbourne. While mother Lea went with Delta, 'the boys' — father Denis and brother Trent — stayed at home in Sydney with the Goodrems' two golden retrievers. Although the family reunited regularly, it was a massive wrench for Delta and she was wracked with guilt that her career had caused the people she loved to live apart.

"I'm a lot **more assertive** than people think."

Delta

She described the split as a 'huge sacrifice' for her family. Sometimes, over-tired from long hours on the set of *Neighbours* and putting *Innocent Eyes* together, the thought of that sacrifice would reduce her to tears. 'I feel so lucky my mum moved from Sydney to Melbourne to be with me and to look after me. It was a big deal for her to do that, leaving Dad and Trent behind. Mum is just amazing.'

'Delta found it really, really hard to be away from home,' says a friend sympathetically. 'She absolutely adores her father and brother. But I never heard her complain. She was such a professional.'

Lea and Delta set up home in a luxury apartment building in Port Melbourne, overlooking the water. When they first moved in they didn't have any furniture, so Delta turned the lounge room into a dance floor with her only possession from Sydney, her stereo. In time, they made it as homely as possible with animal-print cushions and elegant white furniture. Delta and her mother decorated her bedroom in princess-style pinks and purples, and brought her favourite teddies and photos from Sydney.

They kept to themselves in the building, but Delta occasionally set off the fire alarms because she lit so many candles. And in a signal of her growing international life, Lea bought three clocks and set them at different time zones so they could manage international interviews and meetings with music producers.

Talking of the family's split, Lea recalled poignantly that they prised the lounge suite and some bits and pieces from the Goodrem house in Sydney. 'The boys were reluctant to give us anything because they were afraid we would get too settled.'

Homesickness for her family home mingled with the excitement of starting on *Neighbours* and the new focus on her singing career. 'I really miss my dad and my brother and my dogs,' Delta said about the move in an interview at the time. 'And I feel bad for Mum, because she misses them a lot too. But we see each other whenever we can. There's nothing better than going home to be with the whole family.'

It seemed the sacrifice was worth it. On set, the producers were keen for their new character to demo a song on screen, which would then be released to the general public. It was perfect cross-marketing synergy but, of course, when these plans were revealed, she was immediately seen to be following the fortunes of Holly Valance, Natalie Imbruglia and Kylie Minogue.

'I was signed to Sony before *Neighbours*,' she pointed out endlessly in media interviews at the time of her casting. 'I'm a singer first and foremost,' was another refrain, pointedly dispelling the soap-star-turned-singer vibe Wheatley had anticipated. 'There's plenty of room for everyone and everyone has their own style of music.'

In response to *Neighbours*' request for a song, Delta offered up *Born To Try*, which she had just freshly penned at her family home with songwriter Audius Mtawarira only days before moving to Melbourne and starting *Neighbours*. They had already written three songs in the song-writing session and were tossing up whether to go for a swim or write another song. Delta, the workaholic, chose to continue writing.

Talking about the birth of the song, Delta says, 'Audius told me to sing whatever came into my head, or to imagine I was at the Grammy Awards and singing something that made everyone start clapping in the middle of the song. I was thinking, All right, all right, I can do this.'

The phrase 'born to try' crystallised. Musing over those three words, with a dictaphone in her hand, was one of the defining moments of her life. It fused her work ethic, gift and determination with this great opportunity, and created one of Australia's biggest hits, cementing her future career.

She later said the song had her 'heart and soul' in it, and she regards it as the most autobiographical of any she has written. It was true to her, and this time, using the launch pad of a TV show, the truth shone through.

'It's about life, making the right choices and not being scared to go where your heart takes you,' Delta says of the song. At the time she was feeling very emotional and unsure if she would make it. But then her focus kicked back in and all those feelings poured into her song writing. She wrote in the song's lyrics that there was no point dwelling on what she should have been.

'It's really personal,' she reflects. 'I'd been up and down with my music. One day I thought, Well, I'm not born to win and I'm not born to lose, but I am here to give it a good shot.'

The song too was almost therapy for Delta. As she wrote it, she says, 'I felt like I was washing off what happened with *I Don't Care*. I don't want to ever turn bitter because there are a lot of things that can easily bring you down. So I put that aside and started thinking about doing everything that I believe in, going by the rules I've been taught. I was in my room at home when the line "protected by the walls of love" came about. That song didn't come out of nowhere.'

A friend who was one of the first to hear *Born To Try* was blown away too. 'From the moment we heard that first scratchy demo, everyone knew that Delta had found her own style. It was so different, and she sang it so beautifully. And there was no doubt it would be a huge hit.

'Delta loved the song, but had no idea what it was going to do for her. I never heard Delta say it was great, this is it, I'm going to make it. She never had that confidence. Because she is such an utter perfectionist, she would do the vocal takes over and over again.'

Neighbours loved the song too. 'We thought it was sensational, and wrote it into the script,' declares Stanley Walsh.

'They thought the song was perfect for Nina because she's so shy. So it was nice to have that connection with Nina. It was special,' Delta says about *Neighbours*' reaction to the song. Everything seemed to be falling into place.

But first, before its release, Delta had to establish herself on the soap. Initially billed as a guest star, she signed a two-year contract, and within five episodes her role was credited as permanent. She joined a cast of veterans and new actors who worked on a 'kitchen sink' soap that often churned out an episode a day.

Michelle Ang, Patrick 'Paddy' Harvey and Jay Bunyan had joined just before her. She was among the first to welcome her new on-screen love interest, Jaime Robbie Reyne, when he later joined the show. She was heartened by the way the *Neighbours* cast welcomed her into their 'family', and grateful not to be the only new person on set among such a tight group of crew and cast.

'They are great fun, and joining with them made the experience not so scary,' Delta said of her new co-stars. 'When someone new comes in, they welcome them with open arms.'

'She was super friendly and seemed very professional. Down to earth,' says Ben Michaels of his first meeting with the star.

“It’s really personal. I’d been up and down with my music. One day I thought, Well, I’m not born to win and I’m not born to lose, but **I am here to give it a good shot.**”

Delta

Stanley Walsh is just as glowing. 'She was utterly charming and everybody loved her on set. With her talent and beauty, you would think there would be a lot of envy. But Delta was such a nice person, I think people rise above that.'

She filmed many scenes with Kate Keltie, who plays Michelle Scully. 'We just clicked,' Kate said at the time. 'And because you work together all the time, you really get to know the people you work with.'

When they filmed scenes of the love triangle between them, Delta and Kate revealed how they would often wonder how they would feel if they betrayed each other in real life. 'It wasn't easy being nasty to Delta. It's really funny, because sometimes when they call cut we're like, "I'm sorry!" because you start to feel bad. It was strange sometimes pretending not to like each other when we are such good friends.'

Ian Smith, who plays Harold Bishop, also became a friend through a mutual love of music. To Delta's delight, the cast took a keen interest in the crafting of her CD and she often played them tracks she'd recorded for 'market research'.

But the person she became closest to was Blair McDonough, just as she had secretly longed for when she first joined the set. Delta's main focus was her career, but she was still a teenager who dreamed of romance. Blair was now no longer a magazine crush, but part of her new life.

With Blair McDonough, the attraction was mutual. As her co-star and a Morrissey Agency stablemate, he offered to show her around Melbourne. 'He turned red when he saw me,' Delta says of her first meeting with the former *Big Brother* runner-up. She later fondly described him as a 'great big dag'. Just like her, in fact.

While they were genuinely attracted to each other, it was quickly realised that a celebrity coupling doubled Delta's chances of being noticed by the press. Predictably, their unexpected romance delighted gossip writers as they were spotted around Melbourne.

Delta herself kept coy about the romance, saying they had a 'few spontaneous moments' during their sightseeing trips. But soon they couldn't contain their affection. An observer who saw them at the Noosa Festival of Tennis remarked of the young couple, 'They couldn't keep their hands off each other.'

Blair was beaming with pride when his new girlfriend performed at the Sheraton Noosa on the piano. 'There were more jaws on the ground than you could count,' he boasted.

It was not the first time *Neighbours* stars had begun a romance. 'Romances on set are part of *Neighbours* history,' agrees Stanley Walsh. 'They are all young and attractive, let's face it. And as long as it didn't get in the way of the show, then we let it flow. Occasionally there would be tantrums and you would have to pull them aside for a chat, but Delta was always professional on set so I never had to do that with her. They weren't on set together that often anyway, because he was a bit older and his character had a girlfriend.'

Because they were involved in different plot-lines, Blair and Delta did not usually act together. An exception was one scene, where they pulled faces at each other between takes. The scene ended up on the cutting-room floor.

Blair has rarely spoken about their romance. 'She's the most beautiful person I've ever met,' he said at the time. 'She's got a heart of gold and a mind like a diamond.'

He was most struck by her genuineness as a person and by her natural beauty. Her level-headed approach to life tempered his own attitude. 'She brings me back to earth quite a bit, which is good,' he said.

He occasionally teased her. Once he pretended he was already in bed and too tired to pick her up from the airport at midnight, but then he surprised her. Delta was so lost in her own world and her midnight yawns that she didn't see Blair walking beside her through the terminal until they'd gone about 50 metres. 'I nearly gave her a heart attack,' Blair said.

For Blair, Delta's attraction was partly that she was not looking to be with him because of his new-found fame. While the actual winner of *Big Brother,* Ben Williams, is now a classic example of 'Where are they now?', Blair managed to leapfrog from reality TV into a legitimate acting career on *Neighbours*.

Blair remarked that, prior to *Big Brother*, he would try to pick up girls with a group of his 'obnoxious bastard' football mates. 'Girls hated us,' he laughed. 'We were a bunch of pathetic losers.' But now the handsome new heart-throb had more girls than he could handle. Girls who were drunk, girls who were fans, girls who wanted him as a trophy . . . 'The girls are the hardest because they are the harshest. You get a lot of people throwing themselves at you,' he sighed. 'It's more of a turn-off than a turn-on.'

But Delta was classy. She was a professional actor, a talented singer and a rising star. He seemed to have found his equal in his new world, and Delta had too. But one was far more focused on the future than the other. 'We get to share a lot of what we do because it is so closely related and that's the best part of it,' Blair said of his relationship with Delta.

'I think Blair was good for her, because having a relationship helped her be a little like a normal teenager and any chance Delta got to be a teenager was fine by me,' reflects a friend, grateful for any chance Delta had to relax. 'But she was so young and naive.'

Delta said Blair was very supportive of her focus and ambition, and often hung out with her while she was practising and writing new songs on the Delta Project. 'He really loves doing the project with me,' Delta told *TV Hits* in a December 2002 interview.

French photographer Serge Thomann remembers how one night Blair and Delta came to his house in Melbourne so he could help Delta practise a song in French for a performance at the annual Bastille Day ball. 'Delta was so dedicated,' he says fondly. 'She practised and practiced the song in French for hours . . . Blair was so bored, he fell asleep on the couch and she was still singing.'

Blair accompanied her to that year's ARIAs and the soap couple happily smiled for cameras on the red carpet. This time, the fans knew her name and she posed excitedly for photographs.

On the eve of the release of *Born To Try*, Delta was yet to make her mark on the public as a singer, even though those who knew her well constantly reassured her that she was not just another one-hit-wonder soapie star in the making. Delta knew her time was coming.

Wheatley told Christine Sams that during the ARIAs ceremony, he leaned over as Kylie Minogue was receiving her awards and said, 'That will be you next year.' Delta replied, 'Bring it on.'

"All you can really do is **work as hard as you can**, so there's no chance you'll look back and say **you didn't do quite enough** to try and make things work."

Delta

CHAPTER 5

Not Me, Not I

She seemed to have only just gone to bed when the alarm clock rang and her mother was making her breakfast. It was another Delta day.

By now she had adjusted to her gruelling schedule and she swore that her twenty-hour days were worth it. She was busy recording her album and working on new tracks; busy rehearsing her scenes, filming and squeezing in promotional commitments for *Neighbours*; busy being interviewed by weekly TV magazines and radio in Australia and the UK.

It was relentless. There was barely time for rest, let alone for seeing her father and her brother in Sydney.

Her ambition came at a cost. The dual commitment to an album release and to her *Neighbours* role doubled her workload overnight. Yet there was one consolation for the sense of exhaustion that at times threatened to engulf her — she found that the routine and relative stability of a TV show like *Neighbours* was welcome relief from the emotional rollercoaster of her music career. The soap was her day job, where she could simply concentrate on the task at hand and not exhaust her creative energy with the passionate emotion she felt for her music career. She could retreat from her music as well as having the chance to sing on set.

Because Delta had left school to pursue her record contract with Sony, she revelled in the fact that *Neighbours* also gave her a social outlet that had been missing since she'd left Hills Grammar. As much as she tried to keep in touch with her school buddies — saying in interviews that they were still incredible friends — she loved the youthful environment of the *Neighbours* set and the chance to hang out with other young actors.

'I go to the set and have a good laugh, and there are some kids around my age, and that's where I'm lucky, that my career did lead me to something like *Neighbours*, because I had to leave school when I got the album deal,' Delta explained. 'Because we're all around the same age, we are taking the same, scary steps. You spend so much time with those guys that they filter into real life. We are lucky.'

'I think she was lonely before *Neighbours*,' reflected a friend. Delta had been experimenting with different song styles, losing herself in creativity and working on her future. But she had also lost a sense of youth that *Neighbours* gave back to her.

There were other bonuses too. The girl who lived by the rules could go wild at the whim of scriptwriters like Ben Michaels and his team. While Nina was not to be mean, she was growing up, becoming confident, making mistakes and exploring love — just like Delta was. 'Whenever my character does get a bit devilish, I think, Wow! This is exciting! Because I'm a bit boring that way,' Delta says.

On set, either from natural endearing goofiness or lack of sleep from the long hours working on her album, Delta was clumsy. Asked in a *Smash Hits* fan question-and-answer forum what was her most embarrassing blooper on the *Neighbours* set, Delta laughed. 'There's been too many! Once I fell down the stairs onto a set and I was carrying a sandwich plate. Another time, on my second or third day, I knocked over a vase and water went everywhere. They had to stop filming.'

She sang so much around the set that she often disrupted the audio crew, who were forced to tell her to be quiet during filming. She once remarked, even after she became a huge No. 1 star, that 'We still get into trouble if we're mucking about or not learning lines. It is good discipline.' Delta also revealed she got into trouble for changing her hair colour without prior permission. The spontaneous act of pampering — and a rare chance to sit still and relax — earned her a gentle reprimand for disrupting the drama's continuity.

Journalist Cameron Adams describes a memorable moment while in the *Neighbours* green room with Delta. Ian Smith affectionately shouted at Delta to 'shut up' as she leapt over a couch singing Good Charlotte's *Lifestyles of the Rich and Famous*. 'I don't know what was more alarming,' Adams wrote affectionately in his feature for the *Herald Sun*. 'Delta being told to shut up mid-song, or the fact she'd been told off by Australia's nicest man.'

But when she sang on the show, the audio boys couldn't get enough and it was the crew and cast singing along in the background that caused them grief.

The teenager was incredibly happy, and her joy at achieving her dreams fuelled her dedication, commitment and energy. Her relentless capacity for work amazed her producers on *Neighbours*. Peter Dodds, producer, declared that Delta's work ethic was remarkable. 'She has a resilient and positive personality and that's what endeared her to the cast and crew,' he said proudly of his new cast member.

When asked how she coped with her two careers, Delta wasn't joking when she said it was by not sleeping. On average, Delta got three hours sleep a night. While she laughed about her outrageous hours, privately she fretted that her voice was suffering.

Unlike many of her musicians, she did not disrespect her instrument. She was incredibly disciplined about keeping her voice fit with daily vocal exercises. It was yet another thing to fit into her ridiculously full day. She filmed all day on set, then worked on her album at night at Marlin Studios, Melbourne.

'That girl worked her guts out,' says a friend who was clearly worried about her. 'She pushes herself so hard. She's so vulnerable because, while she has this steely determination, she doesn't have huge self-confidence and is very hard on herself. She wants to please everyone, so she puts herself under this enormous pressure. There were times when she really upset me because to anyone in the room she was amazing, and so beautiful, yet she was her own harshest critic. To me, that's a sign of someone who is missing out on their innocence.'

Others noted Delta's perfectionism and dedication. According to Stanley Walsh, she did not treat *Neighbours* simply as a fame vehicle, but was just as dedicated to her acting as she was to her music. 'Delta was determined to improve. She would sit with the editor — who was totally enamoured of her — and watch her performances and make notes.'

But music was always going to be her first passion, and where the main strength of her talent lay. Her confidence that she was finally on track and that her gut instinct was right was confirmed by a meeting with US Sony executive David Massey. 'He was in Australia seeing new local Sony singers one by one,' says a source. 'Some were just talking to him. Then Delta walked in and sang. He was blown away.'

Massey's confidence in Delta gave further encouragement to Sony to continue letting her create her own future. Delta was allowed to travel overseas to work with expensive internationally acclaimed producers like Rick Wake and Gary Barlow. Another songwriter, Kara Dio Guardi, was flown out from the US especially to work with Delta in Melbourne.

'I heard that Massey told Sony to let her be herself,' says a music industry source. 'And when you see the money thrown at her first album, yes, that is very unusual for a singer with an unsuccessful song to have that support. Something happened to get them excited, whether it was the meeting with Massey or hearing a demo or writing her own songs like *Born To Try*. And, to their credit, once Sony is excited, or they have success with a singer, they go all the way. They do not stop'.

Delta's new position as a top priority talent was confirmed when Massey subsequently organised a meeting in the US with then head of Sony, Tommy Mottola. This meeting took place at the suitably glamorous Beverly Hills Hotel. Delta was accompanied by Denis Handlin, CEO of Sony Australia, and Wheatley. Getting straight to the point, Delta played him a tape of her new song, *Born To Try*.

By all accounts, Mottola was as impressed with Delta as Massey had been, and the powerful music executive gave Delta over two hours of his time. 'It was obvious. If Tommy didn't like my music or anything, I would have been out of there in a second,' Delta said excitedly after the meeting. 'I didn't need to waste his time and he certainly doesn't need to be nice to me.'

The meeting went so well that Delta met Tommy Mottola again in New York at Sony's head office and also was introduced to some of the company's favourite and most prestigious songwriters. For Delta it was an astonishing turnaround. Just a year ago, she had been an obscure struggling artist clinging to her singing after a failed single. A girl with dreams, but no success. Now she was yet to feel the joy of a No. 1, but she had a TV career and was Sony's big local hope.

The meetings with Massey and Mottola confirmed Delta's

focus on the US, a long-cherished dream that beckoned from the future. 'Success in the US is the ultimate goal,' she told interviewers determinedly. But first, Delta had to release *Born To Try* and build her profile on *Neighbours*.

The scene in which Delta debuted *Born To Try* was perfect. Directed by Gary Conway, it captured the essence of Delta and her character Nina. It was set in a community hall, where Nina thinks she is alone, but she begins to sing *Born To Try* and is overheard, revealing her talent to the other characters and, most importantly, the public.

Delta was very nervous before the scene was shot, as she is always before she's about to perform. 'I get butterflies before any performance. I get very nervous,' she says. In fact, if she doesn't get butterflies, she thinks it is a bad sign. But when the cameras rolled, Delta says the song and the performance came so naturally 'she didn't have to think about it'.

'When she filmed the scene, we all had goose bumps,' Stanley Walsh says of the atmosphere on set that day. 'The song was recorded for the album at the same time as for *Neighbours*. There were a couple of minor hiccups, like once we got the wrong version. It was slightly different, but luckily it was noted.'

The song went to air in October 2002, five months after Delta's character, Nina Tucker, was first introduced to viewers. Any doubts about the success of the crossover were laid to rest by the fact that Delta's website had 57,000 hits within the next four weeks.

Former Network Ten executive, Rick Maier, remembers how excited the network was when they heard the production tape of the scene for the first time. 'We all thought it was a knockout. Perfect for the show, and perfect to launch Delta. You never know if

"From the moment she stepped on screen I thought **she was the most incredible girl**. Her song *Born To Try* is out of this world. In the short amount of time she's been on screen, **she has stolen the country's heart**."

Daniel Collopy
Home and Away

Delta celebrates her first No.1 hit with the *Neighbours* cast

Delta, Glenn and Gaynor Wheatley at the 2002 Logies

something's a guaranteed hit, but we definitely knew we were dealing with a star.'

It also silenced those who had criticised the original decision to cast a singer and who had said it was too obvious and ill-advised. As rival show *Home and Away*'s Daniel Collopy commented, 'When I heard that *Neighbours* was getting another singer, I thought it was a bit tired. But from the moment she stepped on screen I thought she was the most incredible girl. Her song *Born To Try* is out of this world. In the short amount of time she's been on screen, she has stolen the country's heart.'

The song was sung on set and became the unofficial *Neighbours* theme song. Giggling, Delta says that the other cast members have now heard the song so much, 'I wouldn't be surprised if all of them never wanted to hear it again.' Not so. 'Delta has a voice touched by angels,' co-star and veteran actor Alan Fletcher proudly heralded on his website diary.

Prior to the song's release, Delta slipped over to Finland to film the clip of *Born To Try*. It was starkly different to that of her debut single in both the style of the song and the more refined and sophisticated vibe of the film clip. For starters, Delta remained firmly covered up. The midriff days were behind her. Revealing her new resolve to control her image (backed up by her mother), Delta was very clear on how she was portrayed on screen in *Born To Try* and subsequent clips. She was still styled, but the song reflected a more sophisticated and modest look.

'It's hard when you put the film clip in other people's hands,' Delta admitted in an interview with *TV Hits*. 'It's hard because I know that I'm marketed like a pop star, but I know how much I do behind the scenes. These are my songs and it can be so wrenching when people tamper with them, because they've got to market them. It's like, "What are you doing?" It's got my name on it. I'm the one who's got my face out there — nobody else has. I'm the one who has to stand up there, so I've got to make sure it's OK.'

With *Born To Try*, Delta insisted on a European feel to the clip and meticulously researched different video directors until she found one she felt would give the song depth and soul. This time, she was going to make sure it stood out from the rest. 'I'm not going to stand in a train station and sing la, la, la,' Delta declared.

She finally settled on Mikka Lommi, a Finnish director. 'I didn't specifically decide to do a clip in Finland,' Delta says. 'But from all the video clip stories I read, this was the clip I liked. However, the director was in Finland. So instead of flying a whole crew to Australia, I thought, Why not just fly me over there? It was really exciting.'

Delta was thrilled with the new sophisticated direction. The film clip was what she would call 'classy' and so was the song. Comparing her first two videos, Anthony Rose agrees that *Born To Try* was definitely more sophisticated, but he does not regret the way *I Don't Care* was filmed. 'When you look at *Born To Try*, it's a powerful ballad so of course, if I had directed that video, it would have been completely different to *I Don't Care* because that was essentially a teen pop song.'

Delta joked that the only problem on the set in Finland was that, instead of calling 'Action!' Lommi would shout 'Go!' . . . 'They'd be yelling, "Go, go!" And I was like, "Go where?"' Delta giggled.

There was only one place that Delta wanted to go: to No. 1. In promoting the single, Delta says she did 24-hour shifts. 'It was Melbourne, Sydney, Adelaide . . . fingers crossed,' she said of the gruelling schedule. But there was no point in not pulling out all the stops. Her parents' words rang in her head: 'If it's worth doing, it's worth doing well.' Delta said she never wanted to look back at this time and think she didn't give it the best shot possible.

'I'd go insane if I was just promoting my music,' she said once when asked how she managed the two careers. But later she confessed, 'Sometimes I don't know how I managed to do two jobs at once . . . I had no idea how hard it would be combining *Neighbours* and music.

'Looking back at starting on *Neighbours* and working on the single and the album, I've had my share of anxious moments as to whether things would turn out for me. All you can really do is work as hard as you can, so there's no chance you'll look back and say you didn't do quite enough to try and make things work.'

Delta remembers that as the release of *Born To Try* got closer, she felt increasingly fraught and on edge. *Born To Try* was released just before Holly Valance's character left the show on air. At the time, Holly Valance was pop's golden girl and much was made of the two soap stars' rivalry.

'The rivalry between Holly and Delta was absolute bullshit — a total and utter beat-up,' says a friend. 'Delta never wanted to be a pop princess like Holly. She wanted to be a serious artist and a global talent. But her mum was very conscious of anyone who might take the spotlight from her daughter.'

Lea needn't have worried. *Born To Try* was released in-store two days after Delta's eighteenth birthday and debuted at No. 3. She had half a glass of champagne all night and spent the morning after her birthday party performing and signing at Castle Towers Shopping Centre.

'I didn't drink at the party because I had to sing the next day,' Delta said. 'I was quite nervous because it was my home, but it was great and I sang two songs. If I do anything like that, I'll sing and get on the piano and just have fun.'

In December, *Born To Try* hit the No. 1 spot on the ARIA chart. Finally, all those dreams were now as real as the ARIA chart on her wall. 'I was so relieved it got there. When it went to No. 1, I was like, "Oh, please, please . . ."' Delta says.

A friend remembers that her relief was so great it tempered the actual joy of the achievement. 'She was thrilled, but she didn't run down the road screaming because of the relief she felt.'

This time, the name at the top of the ARIA chart was hers. She called it a fairytale and, just as she did with the Sony signing, Delta held a private and intimate party to celebrate her success.

But not all those expected by the Goodrems came on the night. Wheatley was invited, but he didn't go. His absence was noted by both Delta and Lea Goodrem – it was a dark premonition of the trouble to come. A source says Higgins and Carter were also invited to the party, despite their claims that they have been overlooked by Delta after she became successful.

With this dream achieved, there was another dream to concentrate on: her album becoming No. 1. Delta always had her eye on another challenge.

After writing the song *Innocent Eyes*, she asked Sony if that could be the title track of her debut album. Sony thought it was perfect. She focused on creating more songs based on her life experience. She wrote songs — when she felt happy, when she felt hurt, and when she daydreamed.

'I love writing about growing up and other life stories. I express myself through my music and write about anything that's happening to me. I want to make sure I take it all in, because it's all about the journey. Instead of writing in a diary, I'm writing songs. These are some of my experiences. Everyone has a way of expressing themselves, whether they want to dance, whether they want to write, whether they want to go play tennis. This is my way of putting things down, so I can escape from everything,' Delta says.

Adding to her confidence in the album was the feedback from international songwriters and producers like Gary Barlow, who worked with the British boy band Take That, and Rick Wake, who produced Celine Dion.

The songwriters who were asked to work with the young star reported back to Sony that they were very impressed with her natural ability and musicality. Barlow, in discussing Delta with the head of Artist and Repertoire, Michael Taylor, was most impressed with her piano playing.

But her favourite songwriter and collaborator was Vince Pizzinga, who co-produced Russell Crowe's wife Danielle Spencer's debut album, and with whom Delta co-wrote the title track *Innocent Eyes*. 'Delta is like a little sister to me,' says Vince of the young star.

From everyday moments, like five minutes staring at two colourful earrings on the wall, to the shattering loss of her 'Aunt Sandra' — a close family friend — to Hodgkin's disease when Delta was seventeen, everything was absorbed into her song writing. The song *A Year Ago Today* was dedicated to her Aunt Sandra and was co-written with Mark Holden. It became a song with special significance on her debut album. 'It's so special to me,' she said. 'Aunt Sandra was a huge influence on my life.'

Delta, who believes in angels, confided once that she feels that her 'aunt' is watching over her, and knows what Sandra would like and what she wouldn't, 'When I was doing pop and stuff, she was like, "That's nice." And her face was saying, "That's awful!" I know she'd be really, really happy with me now.'

It's not the only song where Delta has revealed her emotions. As she released *Born to Try*, she and Blair suddenly split.

It is widely thought that *Not Me, Not I* is about the break-up. It was a classic case of her feeling the passionate highs and desperate lows of life. As she clutched her dream of musical success in triumph, her other dream — of love with Blair — was shattered. Delta has never confirmed that the song is about Blair, insisting people should make up their own minds about the lyrics. She only says *Not Me, Not I* is about 'her first heartbreak'.

While generally open about her feelings with the press, on the Blair question she retained an air of mystery and quiet dignity. She was also squirming with embarrassment as she got her first taste of the press dissecting her personal life. 'It feels strange,' she said once, her shyness surging to the fore. It was the first time she was confronted with private questions, and a taste of the downside of fame that she hadn't really considered. It was made all the harder because she was hurting so much.

Rumours of the break-up first circulated at the time of the 2002 Melbourne Cup. The couple then released a statement via celebrity publicist Maria Farmer. Sticking with her mantra — 'If you can't say anything nice, don't say anything at all' — Delta brightly reassured her fans that Blair was still 'her bestest buddy' and 'they spoke every five seconds'. She said they split because of work pressures. 'We are just soooo busy, that's all. Blair is going to

"She's so vulnerable because, while she has this steely determination, **she doesn't have huge self-confidence** and is very hard on herself."

A friend

do a pantomime, and I am promoting the single.' She said she simply had no time.

'*Not Me, Not I* is about Blair. They call it "their song". Listen to the lyrics — you will realise what happened,' a friend says. She claims she heard that Blair sent a text message that broke Delta's heart. But a friend of Blair's says this isn't true and that he ended the relationship because 'he got frustrated with it being too hard to maintain the relationship with both daughter and mother given their hectic schedules. Blair felt terrible because he loved Delta and wanted to be with her — he cared so much about her.'

Blair is now in love with a school teacher. In what could be seen as a reflection on his immaturity at the time, he says he has 'grown up a lot'. At the time, Blair declared that he wished her all the best with her 'amazing talent'. The co-stars needed to keep it clean and dignified. Delta was privately distraught and channelled her pain into the powerful ballad *Not Me, Not I*.

She co-wrote *Not Me, Not I* with acclaimed songwriter Kara Dio Guardi, who spent two weeks with Goodrem in Melbourne at Marlin Studios while recording her album. 'I was pretty upset, and Kara said, "You've got to write a song about it." It's a song I love to sing, because it's got such a dynamic — real highs, real lows. When I sing it, it makes me feel so much better,' Delta reflects. 'While some people find it helps to talk to friends, I prefer to express my problems through my music. That way, I can turn even a bad experience into a good one.'

The song became one of Delta's favourites on the album. True to her empowering personality trait to focus on the positive, it was she who had the last laugh when *Not Me, Not I* was eventually released to her adoring public. 'I knew as soon as I heard it that it would be No. 1,' says the friend. 'It was amazing.' Just like *Born To Try*, cash registers at music stores across the country rang with the fans buying the truth and honesty of Delta's heartbreak.

It took the couple a long time before they managed to strike a comfortable rapport as friends and co-stars, but now they have overcome the heartbreak and maintain a cordial relationship. 'Sometimes after a break-up they [the actors] get a bit emotional, of course, but Delta never let it interfere — she was as professional as always and you never would have known,' Walsh says of the split.

Delta also would have been influenced by what her mother thought of Blair very early in the relationship. Lea's approval of her boyfriends is important to Delta as she and her mother are extremely close, and she values Lea's advice and opinion over anyone else's.

'I introduce a guy to my parents straight away! I think if they can get through meeting my parents, then they can stay around for a while,' Delta remarked once during an interview.

And, while Lea has never publicly commented on her feelings about Blair, a journalist for the UK tabloid *Sunday Mirror* later reported that, during a meeting with Delta and her mother 'the telly went on to *Neighbours*. Lea pointed to Blair and said, "That's the one she used to go out with. I don't like him."'

'Lea was very supportive of Delta's relationship with Blair,' says a friend. 'But of course, afterwards — what's any mother going to think about her daughter's ex-boyfriend?'

Delta is never one to concentrate on boys, but nonetheless this was the end of one of the defining relationships in her life at the most important time of her life. To heal her heart, she threw herself into her work at an increasingly frenetic pace. When asked about her love life, she joked she was so busy she could only wave as she went by. With mounting tiredness, she said the main problem was changing headspace between her two careers.

'We were pretty much blown away by Delta's workload,' Ben Michaels reflects. 'She had a lot of commitments. Music is a big job on its own. As is being on a television show. We just hoped she wouldn't burn out. She was such a nice, if overworked, kid.'

'It was hard for her because she was so young. She had a full-time acting career and music career, which was all day, all night,' says a friend. 'She didn't have much of a social life and she put in a great deal of work for a solid two years. I found her dedication remarkable.'

She tried to keep 'Nina' and 'Delta' separate. 'But I don't mind. I love what I do. I get so emotionally involved in everything, so passionate about it all, that it takes my energy,' Delta explained. 'I don't like to go to smoky places because of my voice and I can't often have late nights as we have such early mornings on *Neighbours*. That's fine. At the moment, I'm happy concentrating on my career and my friends understand.'

But did they? In one of the few glimpses into her break-up with Blair, just nine months after their relationship began, Delta said, 'It makes it hard to sustain a relationship when Saturday night comes around and all I really want to do is catch up on sleep.'

While she has never revealed the most private moments of her heartbreak, Delta herself said her increasingly frantic lifestyle was the reason she and Blair split. But she had no time to dwell on the painful break-up either. Her mum manned the fax machine that every night rolled out the schedule for the next day, with every hour accounted for. Fan mail mounted by the piano and fans endlessly discussed her on the internet forum of her webpage. The three clocks ticked on the wall.

Whereas other stars partied, Delta talked to her fans and rested her voice. She often went to London for the weekend to promote the single and she did a whirlwind European showcase to Amsterdam. 'We would release her for four to five days to go to Europe to promote,' says Stanley Walsh. 'You wanted to do your best for her, because she has such sensational talent.'

Her mother doggedly kept up with the pace. Lea — sounding as exhausted as Delta by this point — once wearily remarked to a journalist about their ridiculously short international trips, 'We spent more time in the air than on the ground.'

The tours were so hectic, Delta said once, that she was never in a foreign city long enough to enjoy the new surroundings and sightsee. It was a blur of famous cityscapes and tour performances. 'I've done no sightseeing at all,' Delta remarked at the time. 'I jump out of the car and say, "Mum, quick, take a photo!"'

Back in Sydney, to Delta's delight, her proud nanna covered her walls with the growing stack of newspaper clippings about her talented grand-daughter. Lea was thrilled for her daughter's success too, but worried about the relentless schedule. 'Sometimes I think she pushes herself too hard,' Lea quietly admitted once.

The force was unstoppable, and even Delta herself was struggling to hang on.

“Delta has the X factor. It’s this ability, without saying a word, to turn heads. Nicole Kidman has it too. You can’t manufacture it, and it can take you a long way.”

Ron Wilson
Network Ten newsreader

CHAPTER 6

Fame

Castle Towers Shopping Centre had never seen anything like it. When their home-grown pop star came to the Centre to do an album signing for *Innocent Eyes*, more than 3000 local fans turned up. The *Hills Shire Times* later marvelled about the scene in an editorial: 'When Delta walked through the shopping centre, flanked by minders, it was almost like watching scenes previously associated with Princess Diana.'

By the time her album *Innocent Eyes* was released in March 2003, Delta had two No. 1 hits: *Born To Try* and *Lost Without You*. Then *Innocent Eyes* went to No. 1 and stayed there for ten weeks. In May, she won a Logie. By June she was a star in the UK with *Innocent Eyes* reaching No. 2 (just denied No. 1 by one of her favourite acts, Beyoncé) and *Born To Try* selling into the Top 5.

The album was to go platinum fifteen times, and has sold over 2.5 million copies. A lot of this success has to do with Delta's relentless promotion at in-store performances and signings at shopping centres.

At the Castle Towers Shopping Centre the fans ranged from five to over fifty. One fan, Jessica Hunt, queued for hours despite a fall at school. Her head bandaged, and due for another serious operation at the Children's Hospital, she collapsed in the line and had to meet her star in a wheelchair. But she said triumphantly it was worth the wait to meet Delta.

Others burst into tears and clutched her hand. Delta felt extremely touched and emotional about the outpourings. Meeting her fans and realising how deeply she had touched some people's lives often overwhelmed Delta and she would find herself in tears. She hugged them and touched them, with one commentator saying that her signings had become a near-religious experience for her young fans because of her impact on them and her own desire to reach out to them and listen to their stories.

Her Sony publicist, used to big rock tours and appearances, was shocked by the explosion of love for the young singer. 'It is insane,' she told equally stunned journalists reporting on the signings.

The fact that Delta has honoured the resolution she made when she was still anonymous — that she would cherish and respect her fans — is responsible for the enormous emotional connection her devotees give back to her. Over half a million fans have contributed to the forum on her website: www.deltagoodrem.com.

She worked closely with her website designers to make sure the site was a true reflection of her, and she gossips on the forums under the signage 'Love and Light', or secretly enters the forum to read and connect. She also prefers to personally release important statements through her website direct to her fans, instead of through the press. She made a surprise appearance at a lunch organised by forum members and regularly writes journal entries to the forum, calling her fans her 'friends'.

This relationship and respect sent her record sales soaring. Her fans — her friends — recognised qualities that those who know her say shines through in person. 'My impression was just the same as everyone else who meets her — natural, unassuming and unaffected,' says Rick Maier.

Most astonishing is Delta's commitment to autograph signings. Whereas most stars, out of shyness or ego, dread meeting the people that made them famous, Delta prioritises it.

After the release of *Innocent Eyes* in March, she signed albums for eight hours straight to ensure everyone who turned up met her and got her autograph. The signing broke a previous five-hour marathon, while other shopping centres were forced to close to other customers because of crowd control.

'I said to her once, "You don't have to do this,"' says a friend. 'And she said, "I know, but I want to."'

'Those eight-hour signings . . . I was with her those days and I'd think, Oh my goodness, Delta,' says Lea, as amazed as everyone else by her daughter's commitment to her fans. 'But as long as you feed and water her, she's fine. But I think those marathon signings are in the past now, because they were too crazy and we have to consider her health.'

Ron Wilson thinks Delta's fame and the instant attraction she inspires in her fans is part of her charisma. 'Delta has the X factor. It's this ability, without saying a word, to turn heads. Nicole Kidman has it too. You can't manufacture it, and it can take you a long way.

'I think it's her song writing too. It gives an insight into her soul, and gives fans a better relationship with her. Being on TV, I know that if people feel a relationship with you — that they know you, and can get inside and hear and feel what you are thinking — then they will have a better understanding and knowledge of you. Kids are going to feel a close connection to her.'

But former *Girlfriend* editor, Sandra Barker, says it's Delta's attitude to her fans which is the force that drives her popularity. 'Teenagers are so impressed with Delta's down-to-earth and caring attitude towards them. They love the fact that she'll spend eight hours signing autographs after a public appearance. Our readers are so inspired by her because they see her as an average teenage girl who has chased her dream and worked hard to see it come to fruition.'

One fan wrote admiringly of Delta that she treated everyone equally. 'It's good that there are some people still like that,' 'Sharon' wrote. 'When talking to her I realised she deserves the world. She is truly one of a kind.'

Delta particularly loved hearing about how people had connected to *Born To Try*. The stories poured into her heart. The song helped her fans through operations in hospital, with one little girl telling Delta that she recovered so much faster than doctors anticipated because she listened to *Born To Try* for inspiration.

Others simply said the song inspired them to follow their own dreams. When her fans wrote to her, Delta read their letters and tried to write back to each letter she received, clearing out her *Neighbours* locker every day. Through letters, signings and on the forum, Delta wanted to connect. 'It was so lovely hearing people give me their own take on my songs. It makes me cry,' Delta says.

The fans use the website to show their love for the singer and compare 'encounters' with her. These are fascinating reading, and show first-hand how the fans appreciate the fact that Delta appreciates them.

One fan described on the forum how she waited to see celebrities at the *Ned Kelly* premiere in Melbourne and came away from the red carpet thinking that out of the stars, Delta was the sweetest, nicest girl ever.

'We were sitting on the steps outside the theatre when a really nice car pulled up across the road and someone got out. I didn't really pay it any attention but my friend suddenly yelled, "Oh my God is that Delta Goodrem?????" I looked up and it was her, we were really excited and we ran over to her and begged for a photo. She told us she was running late but let us get a photo with her anyway, she really was a very nice person.' Later that night, the girls were still waiting to see their stars and Delta gave them an autograph.

Amazingly, with so many signings, Delta still remembers fans. A shy girl called Josie Smart wrote on the website that she has met Delta three times and once Delta gave her a hug and a kiss. 'I held out a card I made, and my LWY [*Lost Without You*] single. I yelled out to her, "Hi Delta," and she said "Hello," and I asked her if she remembered me from Highpoint two days before, and she did! She signed my LWY single, and then signed my friend's BTT [*Born To Try*] single, and then we gave her a card. Every time, she was so down-to-earth and nice!'

Despite her new level of fame, Delta held onto her experiences of everyday life, even though this was getting harder to do. She treasured her moments of peace when she composed new songs, especially during her hectic whistlestop promotional tours overseas.

There were times when she tried to be as normal as her teenage fans. She was grateful that her mum nagged her to eat healthy food and clean up her room. She danced with her headphones on in her room and went for a bike ride or slipped out for a jog in the foggy dawn of Melbourne. She stopped at the corner shop near their building to buy milk and bread, where she and her mother befriended the owners of the store.

She joked she could no longer go out without make-up or wearing her daggy track pants lest she be photographed looking less than glamorous. 'I really, really worried about her,' says a friend. 'She was totally overwhelmed. She lived in a cocoon of her own image. It was all about her singing and her acting. At times she felt she wanted the spotlight to turn off. She would sometimes say to me, "I just want to hang out and be a dag and do nothing." But she was so determined to be the best, she never really relaxed.'

At Christmas, she gamely shopped for presents for her family and scribbled autographs. A fan called Ruthie wrote on Delta's website about her encounter on the festive night: 'I saw her doing Christmas shopping on Christmas Eve. I passed her a few times and she was always talking to like five people. She seemed genuinely nice and probably happy to have some time off catching up with all her friends. She seems to be everybody's best friend cuz [sic] I've talked to like three different people all saying their friend is best friends with Delta Goodrem. Hehe . . .'

At a Christmas concert in Canberra, she was the centre of rehearsals with the *Big Brother* stars and won their hearts by making up risqué lyrics to *Away in a Manger*, playing on her piano specially brought over from Dresden. Although she hadn't yet scheduled a concert tour, her live performances added to her critical credibility, which had been firmly established by the release of *Born To Try*.

Any last lingering thoughts that she was just another soap-star-turned-singer were finally dismissed by a UK music writer, who said, 'Delta should be taken more seriously than the forever stripping Holly [Valance].' A friend remembers he was most struck by Delta's rising star ascendancy over Holly Valance when she and Holly appeared in Melbourne, at the lighting of the city's Christmas tree. A young fan announced loudly, 'Holly's finished.'

At the 2003 Logie Awards, Delta sang live and, according to one observer, was the only one with the 'guts' to do so. Her performance was outstanding. 'She had a problem with an earpiece,' says

Ron Wilson admiringly. 'She kicked off her shoes and kept going. Her ability to cope is just beyond the norm.'

To her embarrassment, her acceptance of her Best New Talent Award that night for the role of Nina Tucker was not so polished. The beautiful beaded dress by celebrity designer Collette Dinnigan ripped as she stood up to accept the award. 'I stood up at the table and felt this rip,' she laughed. 'I thought, Oh, no! Of all times for the dress to tear.' Her good humour about the situation won her more fans on the night. She says the Logies were another dream come true.

To Delta, her performance at the Logies and the critical and popular acclaim she received in the wake of *Born To Try* indicated the essence of why she was famous. Being famous was not her motive. She wanted to sing and perform, and any successful singer and performer would of course be a celebrity.

'I wouldn't be happy not to do this!' she exclaimed once. 'I feel like I want to have a career and I don't feel like I'm missing out on anything. I just feel that I've got some different life experiences that I can share with people.'

But such connection with her fans did come at a price: privacy. While the Australian news media raved about her, and so far she had been spared the indignity of kiss-and-tells, Delta did encounter fans at every turn.

Delta craved time alone with her family. Precious moments with friends and family were often interrupted by fans. She had given so much of herself in person and through her songs, she had asked people into her life so openly and honestly, that the precious privacy line was far more blurred with her than with any other star.

She desperately tried to be accommodating. She excitedly agreed to go to her brother's formal, but instead spent the entire evening fending off fans from her old school. 'I didn't get to see my brother the whole night,' she said. 'Things like that upset me a little bit.'

That night Ron Wilson hosted the formal, at the Sheraton on the Park in Sydney. 'Delta arrived late. And the ballroom cleared to go and see her. She posed for so many photographs with the kids. It was the week before she realised she was sick. She must have been buggered, but she still had time for the people she grew up with.'

Yet despite the pressure, she insisted she was lucky. She was so, so lucky — it was all good. 'I am living the dream I've wanted since I was a little girl,' Delta insisted.

She was aware that her passion to be a singer would bring fame from an early age, but for Delta it was a passion to perform, not pose, which drove her on. 'From five years old she wanted to perform, and does a five-year-old have a concept of fame? She wanted to make people smile, to sing and make them happy. I think she wanted to please people, really,' Lea says of her daughter's need to sing.

Delta said she pitied those who craved to be a celebrity for the sake of it. 'You know when people want to be famous for the fame? I don't understand that. I love talking to people, so when people come up to me in the street it's like I just have a chat and say, "Hi". It's been a progression from doing TV shows, growing up and always having people around me. My fame is not an issue — I don't even think about it. I just accept it and get on with it.'

Those who know Delta say they are immediately impressed by

her natural personality, and the dizzying success of *Born To Try* did not create a monster. 'With that incredible success — a star on TV and a star with music — it never went to her head,' says Stanley Walsh proudly. 'And of course over the years I have seen people's egos bloom. It's a very seductive thing at sixteen or seventeen to be a star, but it's normally those who are not so successful as Delta or Holly, who was very sweet on set and down-to-earth too. If you ever have a daughter — and I do have one who is very nice — you would want her to be like Delta,'

Wendy Stapleton, brought in to play Nina's mother on air, met Delta at the height of her popularity and just before her dramatic departure from *Neighbours*. In the three weeks they worked together, Wendy said Delta was 'just the same as most teenagers in her hopes and wishes for the future. Of course, there is the fact she is on every magazine cover so it makes it hard to be the girl next door.'

Professionally, Michael Taylor has watched Delta become a sophisticated young woman in control of a fantastic talent. 'She's really matured and grown up in past years,' he said in a *TV Hits* interview about his time with the star. 'She was signed to Sony when she was only fifteen. Although she was writing songs at that time, I don't think she had the voice to really put strong lyrics behind them. But over the past couple of years, she really has learnt how to structure a song and also what she wants to say within the confines of a song.'

Sue Williams was equally intrigued when she met Delta during an exclusive interview for Lea and Delta's preferred publication, *The Australian Women's Weekly*. 'Much of Delta's charm lies in the natural way she presents herself — the youthful enthusiasm is never overlaid by false sophistication,' Sue observed in the exclusive. 'She may look like a gorgeous, alluring woman on the outside, but inside she's still just a starry-eyed teenager.'

The most famous teenager in Australia also collects fairies, brought her teddy bears to Melbourne, and still wants to believe in Santa. 'She does seem so sophisticated, but there are times when she seems like a young girl,' a music industry source agrees.

Delta giggled when she confessed to an interviewer that her favourite joke was 'Why did the chicken cross the road?' She craves Cadbury's Top Deck chocolate and she loves the sounds of her dogs barking when she gets home.

Ambulances make her feel afraid, the news makes her cry, and she has a phobia about sharks, so she hates swimming at the beach. 'I get bored doing nothing, anyway!' she laughed about her fear of the water. She loves watching *The Jetsons* cartoons and 60s TV shows like *Bewitched* and *I Dream of Jeannie*.

A friend is continually astonished that such sophisticated and soulful song writing can come out of a teenager who loves teddies. 'What always struck me about Delta is that she is such a little girl but she wrote these emotionally mature songs. She has an astounding song-writing ability. She would read out these songs to me at sixteen and I would look at her and think, where is this coming from? She has such an emotional well underneath the innocence and naivety.'

New Idea's astrologer, Karen Moregold, researched Delta's chart based on the planetary activity on the day she was born. A fascinating picture of Delta emerges, which many would recognise as the personality of Delta today and also the personality guiding such insightful creativity.

'Her star sign is not only Scorpio, but she has Saturn and Pluto in Scorpio,' Karen explains of the powerful combination guiding Delta's personality. 'This means she has a resolute will and an intense, fighting spirit and she internalises her emotions and experiences — she is a very deep and reflective personality. Along with the Scorpio is Venus, Neptune, Mercury and Uranus in Sagittarius, which points to an extremely artistic and sensitive nature, yet not afraid to take risk, and loves new challenges and stretching the boundaries of her talent. She has a vision, is progressive and has a positive, resilient spirit.

'Another feature of her horoscope is the moon in Taurus, from this her strong family values and loyalty stems, and a strong need for financial and emotional security. This colours her judgment to take risks — she keeps her feet on the ground. She is a contradiction, because the Sagittarius is so sunny and positive, but the Scorpio gives her that insightful and soul-searching capability which comes through in her songs. She is a very complex person because there are so many levels to her nature.'

Even after achieving massive fame, her friend says she retained her endearing innocence and vulnerability. 'As she got closer to eighteen, she started to spread her wings and become more independent, and being on *Neighbours* and her singing success helped too. She started to enjoy being a celebrity and to be more confident. But she was still a little girl and retained that innocence. She still had her pink clothing, pink bedroom, her bears and chocolate and her adoration of her family.'

Delta herself says there is a 'little girl' inside, and the song *Innocent Eyes* is about her maturing, protected by her close family and high morals. The song, co-written with Vince Pizzinga, was the

Delta and Blair in a fashion shoot for *Girlfriend*

Delta at the 2003 Logies

"Our readers are so inspired by her because they see her as an average teenage girl who has chased her dream and worked hard to see it come to fruition."

Sandra Barker
Former *Girlfriend* editor

one she most desperately wanted to succeed because it was such a personal song.

But this little girl also has a highly developed awareness about her image and her position as a role model to young girls, which tempers any immature behaviour in public. 'Delta set out to inspire people,' Wheatley has said of Delta. 'She wanted to be a role model.'

'To me being a good person is something that is such an important thing to portray. To be a decent human being is important. I want people to connect to that. There's no shame in saying, "This is who I am,"' Delta says of her goodness-by-name, goodness-by-nature image. But revealing the steel under the sweetness of her personality, she added she does not consider the Joneses when she is making decisions. This is her life and, as she often repeats, you only have one shot.

Many people are amazed to be reminded how young Delta still is because she seems so mature, successful and so dignified for a girl of such a young age. While most of her professional peers are endlessly falling off the rails via eating disorders, pornographic videos on the web, plastic surgery and 24-hour quickie marriages in Vegas, Delta attracts headlines that are fascinating but rarely undignified. Her news is one of outrageous success, awards, personal challenges and high-profile romances that don't descend into sleaze.

She cites as her own role models glamorous, sophisticated women like Nicole, Charlize Theron and Olivia — women who have overcome personal challenges such as divorce, childhood traumas and cancer to earn huge admiration from the public.

'She was always very mature,' reflects Stanley Walsh. 'By eighteen, she seemed to me more like twenty-four.' Delta herself realises her public behaviour often belies her age. 'At times I seem more mature than I am,' Delta reflects. 'It's just because I'm around adults all the time.'

A source says that Delta was babysat once in Europe, where she and her band were to do a promotional showcase. 'I heard that she was just like a teenager,' shrugs the source. 'She really didn't say that much at all and you could tell she was into clean living — she didn't want to go out and party.'

Her clean image was emphasised when answering questions from eager fans for a *Girlfriend* magazine feature. Delta was asked for advice on the question of the drug Ecstasy. 'Dear Delta: I love going to dance parties with all my friends. Some of them take Ecstasy and I want to try it but I'm scared.'

Delta, the role model, answered, 'I can tell you right now, taking Ecstasy is not a good idea. I personally have never touched drugs or cigarettes, and I don't feel like I'm missing out on anything. If you are a friend, you'll tell your pals it is not a good decision — it's not going to bring anything to your lives except harm. You can have lots of fun in other ways.'

You could hear the sighs of relief from mothers all over Australia. Because she is such a positive role model, the parents of some of her youngest fans are happy to wait patiently in the manic queues for their little girls to meet their wholesome idol, buying yet more records for their adoring daughters.

'Most people go the other way, but maybe people are now looking for good, clean entertainment. Almost a rebellion against a rebellion. Look at Guy Sebastian,' comments Ron. 'He got out there on *Idol* and said he wasn't promiscuous, and he won. Kids and parents can take Delta and Guy as role models.'

'While some famous teenagers take part in harmful activities, it's so refreshing to have Delta, who respects her mind and her body and has gained success by being true to herself,' says former *Girlfriend* editor, Sandra Barker. Former *Total Girl* editor and now *Girlfriend* editor, Sarah Oakes, says even the youngest girls idolise Delta. 'They love Delta because they can relate to her. When they stand in front of the mirror and sing into their hairbrush, they dream of growing up to be her.'

She also stood out for dressing stylishly, but relatively modestly. Asked about her favourite dress, Delta said it was black and came down to her knees. She only finds her back sexy. Whereas Holly flaunted sexuality to help sell records, Delta recoiled from Holly's image and said she couldn't pull it off, even if she wanted to. She'd learned her lesson with the failure of *I Don't Care* that sexy didn't suit her.

In her few comments about Holly, Delta earnestly assured interviewers there was no rivalry between them and Holly congratulated her at the Logies. But she is blunt about their opposing views on using sex to sell records.

'She may take her clothes off to be sexy, but I will never go naked. That's not who I am. I'm not shy, but I think sexy is not about flaunting. I don't even like wearing miniskirts, and you won't catch me wearing hotpants!' Remembering her 'If you can't say anything nice' motto, she hastily added, 'But they look great, good luck to them.'

The editor of *TV Hits*, Fiona Wright, observed that one of the reasons teenage girls love Delta is that she has an ability 'to succeed without shedding her clothes'.

Proving the old adage that it's best to leave something to the imagination, in 2004 Delta was voted Australia's sexiest woman in the annual '100 Sexiest Women In The World' poll conducted by the young men's magazine *FHM*. Delta was astonished, but graciously accepted the 'honour'.

'I don't really think of myself as sexy but I'm very humbled,' Delta said. Winning more points with her fans, most of whom are young and vulnerable with shaky self-esteem, Delta the role model added, 'I really believe women are sexy in their own way. It has a lot to do with inner beauty, and feeling good and confident about yourself.'

But the men's magazines will be waiting a long time before she considers any sexy shoots. 'It is non-negotiable,' says a friend. 'She has a high moral code. And she knows she doesn't have to wear a bodysuit to sell records like Holly.' Delta herself said that, for now, she wants her records to sell themselves. 'Maybe in ten years time,' she said of doing a raunchy photo shoot. 'But my gut instinct tells me not to.'

She once tellingly responded to an interviewer that she may one day reinvent herself into a wild child. Madonna and Kylie have survived decades in the pop industry by radically changing their images, and Kylie earned valuable street cred during her romance with rock legend Michael Hutchence. Delta has repeatedly said she is looking for a career with longevity.

Can she stay wholesome and pure and still retain her fans as they mature too? She knew one day she would need an edge, and said she was looking forward to exploring her 'darker side'.

But her first dramatic change of image came about through something more frightening and traumatic than she could have ever imagined.

"In a matter of a few seconds, my whole world turned upside down. I was suddenly very cold. I couldn't stop shaking. I felt like a little animal that had been backed in a corner."

Delta

CHAPTER 7

Extraordinary Day

With a security guard by the door and flowers piling up in the living room, Delta was at home shaking with shock and crying in the arms of her father, mother and brother.

'I was so upset when they told me. So upset,' she said of her cancer diagnosis. 'Completely shocked. But deep down, despite the shock, I wasn't actually surprised.'

Delta had first put the ominous fatigue down to her gruelling schedule, as did Lea. 'Her mother blamed herself for not discovering it earlier,' says a friend sympathetically. 'She thought it was because she was working so hard, that of course she would be tired. You don't think it would be cancer.'

While there was concern Delta would burn out, nobody could have foreseen such a serious illness. Hinting at the strain she was under in the lead-up to her cancer diagnosis, Delta said that *Neighbours* was very supportive of her on set despite her exhaustion. 'If you rock up to work and you're tired and agitated or you snap at someone, then they're instantly going to know why because they know what you're dealing with.'

In the wake of the diagnosis, it wasn't long before the obvious question was asked: Had Delta's massive workload, and the stress she was under, accelerated or even caused her cancer? 'There is a general sense in the community that stress causes cancer or at least contributes to it,' explains Melanie Price, who is completing a PhD in psychological medicine at the University of Sydney and has specifically researched the link between stress and breast cancer. 'The precise biological pathways are unclear, but chronic stress does affect the immune system. Therefore the body has fewer resources to fight any changes, such as the progression from pre-cancerous to cancerous.

'There is usually no single cause of cancer. It's more multiple — family history, genetics and environmental exposure all increase a person's risk. My personal view is that it's extremely high levels of stress or prolonged stress that breaks the camel's back. Your diet and sleep is affected . . . It's like a royal flush of factors and stress is one possibility to push you over the limit.'

Ms Price says that while stress alone will never cause cancer, there is a theory that those who bottle up their anxiety and suppress their emotions have a cancer-prone personality, particularly when they suffer additional stress. 'If Delta is a perfectionist and never complains; if she is usually stoic, holding in her anger and frustration and unaware of the turmoil inside her; then she might well fit the picture of a cancer-prone personality.'

But Delta, while prone to nerves, perfectionism and stoicism, has incredible family support and is loved as much for her positive spirit as for her talent. It's well known that a positive approach to life and challenges can make massive differences to health.

As the months passed, apart from the fatigue, Delta noticed alarming physical signs that things were perhaps not 'all good' after all. A mysterious rash spread over her body, which she now knows was her immune system breaking down. In her exclusive interview with *The Australian Women's Weekly* about her cancer fight, Delta said she attributed the rash to being completely run-down.

She became thinner, and to combat the exhaustion, began eating more carefully and finding time to exercise, which had always made her feel better in the past. But then she found a lump above her collarbone, at the base of her neck, while working out at the gym. 'I'd found this lump and pushed any negative thoughts to the back of my mind but my imagination was racing,' Delta said later. The lump, which she found in February 2003, grew along with her work schedule.

By July, she was in a severe state of exhaustion and frequently waking in the night with feverish night sweats. The simplest tasks seemed impossible. She tried to maintain a sense of normality and invited friends over for dinner. She ended up hopelessly burning the dinner and almost in tears. In the end, she ordered pizza.

Yet while personally she was on the verge of collapse, her continuing success gave her the motivation to keep pushing her dream forward. There was also no question of leaving *Neighbours*. She had agreed to a two-year contract — that would have seen her through the launch of a follow-up album to *Innocent Eyes* — and she loved the show.

Asked by *Smash Hits* magazine if she had a 'see you later' attitude to *Neighbours* now she had her musical success, Delta answered, 'I hold *Neighbours* in the highest regard and I am so thankful to them forever. I didn't know my path was going to lead there and I'm really lucky I did coz [sic] now I have a family that will look after me forever.'

Delta was in bed when the news came through that *Innocent Eyes* was No. 2 in the UK. 'The phone started going haywire. I was like, "Great, good to hear." Then I went to sleep. I was really tired.' The success and exhaustion were so overwhelming that Delta could no longer react in the way she once thought she would. She just wanted to go to bed.

'Maybe it will hit later,' she said, poignantly puzzled by her own lack of excitement. She had everything she had ever dreamed of, bar success in the US. Why wasn't she feeling on top of the world?

Her worried mother confided to journalists how tired the

"If Delta is a perfectionist and never complains; if she is usually stoic, **holding in her anger and frustration** and unaware of the turmoil inside her; then she might well fit the picture of **a cancer-prone personality.**"

Melanie Price
Psychologist

teenager was. Despite her exhaustion, Delta still went ahead and did a huge six-song live showcase at Channel [V] studios in Sydney. She looked beautiful in a pink Kirrily Johnston dress, now known as the 'pink bunny' dress because of its diamond-encrusted halter straps. Her hair was in a simple ponytail, and she drank water throughout the performance and brightly chatted with fans crammed into the audience.

During a promotional visit to Brisbane, her publicist in Queensland noted how exhausted she looked and tried to make a joke of it by saying she could have a great holiday when she was twenty-five. Delta didn't find it funny.

There was no opportunity to rest. This was her time and, as she had vowed, no matter how wretched she felt she refused to sit back and not give it her best shot.

With three No. 1 singles in Australia, two Top 5 hits in the UK and the album *Innocent Eyes* also a success in Europe, Delta was focusing on the US. She was due to fly to New York to start intensive planning for the release of her album to the US market, with the first single slated for release at the start of the following year.

In the days before the diagnosis, Delta visited some seriously ill children at Ronald McDonald House at the Royal Children's Hospital in Melbourne. She felt awkward, as she always did when confronted with children who were desperately ill. She kept up a smile for her delighted, frail fans, masking her own exhaustion. Delta didn't realise how soon she would come to understand their trauma first-hand.

In *The Australian Women's Weekly* exclusive written by Michael Sheather, Delta spoke hauntingly of the night she knew something was seriously wrong. The evening in Melbourne started in a relaxed way. She went out for dinner with friends, then went to sleep just after midnight for her 5.30 am start the next day on the *Neighbours* set. It was one of the few times she and her mother were apart.

At 3.31 am, Delta awoke bathed in sweat. 'I woke up completely soaked and I'd had a bad dream,' she told the *Weekly*. 'All I saw was the Grim Reaper. It was so prominent in my mind, so vivid. All I remember was this dark face and — I know this sounds awful — a grave. I froze. I was lying there and thought, My God, there's a bad spirit in the house. Or someone was in the house. Something terrible was about to happen.'

It was a premonition. 'That is very unusual,' comments Professor Phyllis Butow, from the University of Sydney. 'Maybe she was starting to feel symptoms that made her feel unwell.'

Terribly distressed, Delta called her mother, then rang her close friend Jude Bolton and spoke to him for an hour. Incredibly the next day, 4 July, Delta still went to work and hid her panic and exhaustion from fans visiting the set. She even managed to serenade them with *It's Raining Men*. 'She was hugging us and didn't seem sick at all,' said twelve-year-old Olivia Whelan. 'She seemed happy, cheerful and really lovely.'

Delta dragged herself onto a plane and, when she arrived home, fell into her mother's arms. Lea urgently organised a specialist to see her for checks. The symptoms that had plagued her for months were classic of cancer: recurring night sweats, fatigue and weight loss.

The biopsies were traumatic for Delta. 'I am phobic of needles and I had, like, four,' she says. Delta was so upset and frightened she fainted during the biopsy. A small white strip of plaster covered her delicate neck afterwards and was duly noted by the press. She

"**I will be back** just as soon as my treatment is completed. Knowing I have **your love and support** is making a huge difference ."

Delta

said they were just routine tests and that she was run down. She was relentlessly upbeat and said, 'Everything will be fine.'

While Delta waited for her results, she turned to her world of music and her looming trip to the US. 'She was excited to be back in the studio,' Vince Pizzinga said of those last days of innocence. She wearily celebrated being No. 1 in Australia and No. 2 in the UK. She was particularly thrilled for co-writer Vince that her debut album's title track, *Innocent Eyes,* had also gone to No. 1. 'I felt like an angel telling him,' she says.

But Delta later revealed that every time she triumphed, she felt physically worse. She grew to have a love-hate relationship with her success. 'Every time I have a No. 1 — that is when I've felt sick,' she admitted candidly in an interview after her treatment.

She was working in Vince's North Sydney studio on the day of her medical test results. It was Tuesday 8 July, five days after her terrifying dream. Delta recalled the door of the studio opening, and she looked up to see her family and Vince. As she did so, the innocence drained from her eyes as the truth of the diagnosis was reflected in their agonised expressions.

'Suddenly I could feel my heart beating and the blood pounding in my ears,' Delta said in the *Weekly* article. 'I looked at them and then at my song-writing partner, Vince. There were tears rolling down his face. When I looked back, Trent was crying. And I started to cry.

'Everything started to swirl. Mum put her arms around me. I could hear Vince saying, "It's OK sweetheart. Everything will be all right." The enormity of that moment, hearing those words from Mum, was overwhelming. In a matter of a few seconds, my whole world turned upside down. I was suddenly very cold. I couldn't stop shaking. I felt like a little animal that had been backed in a corner. I kept thinking, My God, I am eighteen, this is not supposed to happen. I was sobbing. All the way to the hospital. I was shaking and it didn't stop for 24 hours.'

Lea took charge. She called Sony, *Neighbours* and of course Wheatley, who was in the US. With rumours already intensifying that Delta was ill and had a lump, the family also had to deal with how to tell Delta's fans that she was ill before the speculation really got out of hand.

A family insider claims that Lea and Delta, already in fragile states because of the cancer diagnosis, were upset when Wheatley suggested they wait until he returned to Australia so he could do the announcement as a press conference by her bedside. They were also upset that it was three weeks before Wheatley saw Delta once he arrived back in Australia, and friends of the family claim he returned on the flight he'd always been booked on and in fact made no special effort to come back earlier.

But a friend of Wheatley's says that any suggestion he was not thinking of Delta's best interests gives the wrong impression. He was 'absolutely shattered' when he was told that Delta had such a serious illness. 'He is a very emotional man and felt like it had happened to his own daughter,' the source says. 'This is the girl he protected for four years . . . He was totally devastated and so worried. He immediately told Qantas to repatriate him — an emergency flight. He was shut out by the family.'

Delta decided instead to release a statement with a plea for privacy. In this statement her family announced she had Hodgkin's disease — a treatable form of cancer. Delta said, 'I want to assure my fans that I will be fine and I will be back just as soon as my treatment is completed. Knowing I have your love and support is making a huge difference and I look forward to seeing you all soon.' The treadmill, as Delta called her life, had violently stopped.

'People who have been in control of their lives, particularly people who have had a lot of success, find cancer a particularly challenging experience because cancer is uncontrollable,' Professor Butow observes of the challenge Delta faced.

Delta was devastated that her planned launch into the US — her ultimate dream — had been brutally derailed by her health. Just a week before, she had excitedly told fans of her impending trip on her website journal. 'She was shattered she could not go after the US . . . but then she said, "I will do it in a year's time or two years — however long it takes,"' says a friend, proud of her positive spirit.

Delta herself pleaded with her fans, 'Positive thoughts — no sadness allowed.'

At St Vincent's, Denis Handlin visited his sick star and said he found her fragile but concentrating on her music to take away the anxiety. There were lyric sheets spread all over her bed.

In a telling comment, which sheds light on the family's expectations of Wheatley, Denis Handlin said, 'There is a relationship with Delta that goes beyond business.' Delta was comforted and grateful that Denis — the head of her second family, Sony — made time to visit her as soon as he could. The protective net of her mother, her family, *Neighbours* co-stars and crew and her powerful record company was closing around her.

Delta's own neighbours soon realised there had been a dramatic development at the Goodrem home. The quiet streets of Glenhaven had turned into a newsroom. TV vans lined the street. Journalists and photographers crowded their door to try to get extra quotes and reactions for the front-page story the next day. Delta, already reeling from the diagnosis and the ordeal ahead, was now in a media storm. 'Within a few hours of being told by the doctors, my illness was on the news. It was totally crazy.'

Her family were equally stunned. 'Lea especially couldn't understand at first why there was so much interest,' says a friend. Her daughter was ill, it was a private matter and it was going to be front-page news around the country. That was, I think, when they realised just how big a star Delta had become.'

To shield the star, her high-profile friends took the spotlight. Molly Meldrum vowed that she would ultimately triumph in this battle with her health. 'She is a very strong girl. You only have to look at the way she has approached her career so far to see how determined she is. She never says "I'm too tired" or "I can't" — she'll use the same strength and determination to get through.'

Idol judge Mark Holden visited and said he thought it was Delta's 'destiny' to fight cancer. He also could see how her illness was going to have a massive impact on her young fans. 'There are a lot of people, like my daughter who is eight and has Delta's picture on her wall, who are going to be confused by it and are not going to understand what's happened to her,' he remarked.

Mark was right. Parents all over Australia had to explain to Delta's bewildered younger fans why everyone was saying their heroine had cancer. 'They were too young to really understand,' observed Sarah Oakes (who was then the editor of *Total Girl*) about her young audience.

On 19 July, ten days after the announcement, Delta personally apologised on her website to her fans for the shock of how they found out about her diagnosis. 'There was no easy way to let people know. I was trying to come to terms with the news myself, so I'm sorry. Big thanks, hugs and kisses to everyone for your amazing and overwhelming support . . .'

She described the chemotherapy as 'obviously not much fun'. Then Delta the role model wrote, 'I also know there are others in the world worse off than me. I will be out and about in no time. I am determined good things will come as a result of this challenge.'

The Castle Hill area was devastated. Their princess was in peril. The Hills Grammar School fundraised for St Vincent's Hospital in the months after Delta's diagnosis. Her brother Trent and fellow school captain Natasha Evans presented a cheque to the hospital on the school's behalf at Christmas 2003.

Close friends, such as AFL player Jude Bolton, spoke briefly to the press. So too did Vince Pizzinga. Band member Steve MacKay asked everyone to send Delta good vibes. 'The fact she's eighteen and has so much determination, that is the thing I admire about her most. I really want to stress first and foremost that I'm a friend and I just want to send good vibes.' Pleading for Delta's privacy, Steve added, 'I think at this time it is important to give her space to chill out. It's pretty hardcore what she has to do.'

Russell Crowe also put his oar in while performing with his band, 30 Odd Foot of Grunts. Without a trace of irony, the brilliant actor and not-so-brilliant singer said, 'Delta is a gem. In a music business that allows a lot of wannabes under the wire, she can really sing, she writes her own music and she is a stunner.'

Elton John rang privately to tell Delta that Great Britain was behind her, and sent her orchids. Delta didn't believe it was Elton when he phoned and was enormously grateful for his support. She said that, throughout her treatment, Elton seemed to know when she felt at her absolute worst and a gift would then arrive to cheer her up.

And, in a gesture Delta will always treasure, her idol Olivia Newton-John — herself a survivor of breast cancer — also got in touch. 'She's my absolute idol. When news of my illness broke, she sent me the most beautiful letter,' Delta said gratefully. 'I promise you, this is just a blip on the radar,' it began. 'To get that positive message from someone I look up to so much, and who's beaten the illness herself, was just amazing.'

'To have international press on your door, to have international stars calling . . .' Ron Wilson reflects. 'I think that is when they realised how huge Delta was.'

The painful realisation of how newsworthy Delta's cancer was came during one of her first visits to St Vincent's Hospital. An orderly was caught talking to a photographer and was suspected of trying to slip him some pictures.

The hospital was horrified and the orderly was severely reprimanded for his suspicious action, although he denied any dealings with a photographer. A hospital spokesperson at the time said the family were very distressed when told of the incident. 'They couldn't believe anyone would try and breach Delta's privacy while she was undergoing treatment. They couldn't believe anyone would stoop that low.'

Delta's first public appearance was three weeks after her cancer announcement, at the ARIA No. 1 Chart Awards function in Sydney. More casual than the annual ARIAs, but still a prestigious awards event, the awards are presented to chart-topping performers the previous year.

Cancer or no cancer, Delta wasn't missing this awards ceremony. Wheatley was by her side. Despite the tension that was then

“She was terrified about her voice. Utterly terrified. When all you ever wanted was a singing career, this was worst-case scenario . . . Her mortal and professional **life was in danger.”**

A friend

growing between Delta, her mother and Wheatley, Delta — ever the professional — smiled and hugged the press with her manager looking on. She was pale, but wore a determined smile and a soft, dramatic haircut.

Delta's effort in appearing during such a personal health crisis, and her professionalism in front of the cameras during the twenty-minute press conference, astounded the gathered media and industry. It was an emotion-charged high, even though there was a low looming around the corner.

'I've started treatment and it will continue for the next four or five months. I know there will be good days and bad days,' she declared, still relentlessly upbeat. 'On the good days I do what I love to do, and I'm really happy I could get here today.' Delta graciously thanked her fans and her record company for their support, calling Denis her 'second dad'.

Denis Handlin said he was in tears at the Awards watching his young, fragile star. 'I have to say I love her,' Handlin said. 'When she said that about me being her second dad, it was tough to get through. It means a lot. I think we are a family, and I feel very close to her.'

As her inner circle knew, the most frightening discovery was not only that the lump was malignant, but that there were multiple tumours around her throat. The tumours had to be removed as soon as possible, so Delta was rushed into a three-hour operation. But they could not remove all the tumours, and the remaining ones had to be radiated, putting her vocal chords at risk. She also needed chemotherapy.

Delta was terrified for her life and her soul. Would she be able to sing again? There was a real risk that her beautiful voice could die in the treatment process.

Speaking to the *Weekly* much later, Delta said the prospect of losing her voice was the scariest thing of all when confronting her illness. 'I said, "Please don't, this is my life." I needed to have radiation to have a life but there was a risk that it might take away the one thing that made my life the way it is.'

'It was horrendous,' says a friend. 'Horrendous . . . All we cared about was her. She was terrified about her voice. Utterly terrified. When all you ever wanted was a singing career, this was worst-case scenario . . . Her mortal and professional life was in danger.'

Delta knew what lay ahead from seeing her Aunt Sandra, a close friend of the family, suffer. Delta had sung for Aunt Sandra and Uncle George during her many childhood concerts in the family lounge room. Only two years before Delta's diagnosis, Aunt Sandra had died from Hodgkin's lymphoma. 'I saw Aunt Sandra go through her treatment and it was heart-wrenching,' Delta later told *The Australian Women's Weekly*. 'But I didn't want to think about death.'

'Delta's experience of seeing someone close to her go through the treatment — particularly with that outcome — would have intensified fear and anticipation of what was going to happen to her,' says Melanie Price. She would have been a very frightened girl.

She believed in the power of faith. She believed in angels. She thought God had sent her this challenge for a reason. To dwell on death was not Delta's way of dealing with this twist in her story. She concentrated instead on positive, motivating thoughts. And she cried her eyes out.

“She’s so positive. She knows all about the treatment and everything that goes along with it. She has a good head on her shoulders, that girl.”

Jay Bunyan
Neighbours

Delta performing at the 2003 Alan Border Medal.

Delta at the 2003 ARIAs with Lea, Dennis and Trent

CHAPTER 8
Lost Without You

The atmosphere was one of disbelief. The tight-knit cast sat around the *Neighbours* set, stunned and in tears.

Producer Peter Dodds had just told them the news that Delta was seriously ill with Hodgkin's disease. Bluntly, Delta had cancer. She would grow to hate the word.

Ben Michaels succinctly sums it up when he says, 'It was a dark day at the office. We obviously felt for Delta and were very worried . . . We were amongst the first people to know in Australia and we knew it was about to explode in the media.'

'I addressed everyone on the studio floor,' Peter said in the days after the announcement. 'People were naturally shocked, and a bit dazed. We talked about it for a while, and then decided to take a break and finish the day.'

While his cast came to terms with the news, Peter, the other executives and the scriptwriters were torn between anxiety for Delta and the hole in the script her sudden exit from the show created. The news had a massive impact on the future story-lines of the show. There was no question of Delta continuing to work the long hours on the soap she had been doing. 'It was a very intense time,' Ben Michaels remembers.

Walsh says that it is a true mark of Delta's decency that in her darkest hour she still considered others. 'She was very worried how it would affect the show and everyone there. She said, "How will you manage?" It made me want to cry. I told her, "Don't worry darling, you focus on getting better."'

'You never would have known she was so seriously ill,' continues Stanley. 'That's why it came as such a shock, really unbelievable and great concern to everyone. It was so hard to believe with her vitality and clean living — I mean she didn't drink, smoke or do anything silly — that she had such an illness.'

There was no question of Delta continuing to work on the show during treatment. Nina had to be written out, and so the show went into emergency mode. Peter Dodds, Ben Michaels, Stanley Walsh and other executives began re-crafting story-lines to write Delta out in a way that would allow her later return if this became possible. 'We formed a story scrum and determined what the battle plan for the character would be in the immediate future,' Peter Dodds said.

'The executive producers, producers, script writers and editors all were at the meeting,' Stanley Walsh explains. 'Things have suddenly happened before, like accidents or someone would fall over. We had to put Delta to one side and go, Right, how are we going to keep this show going? What is the least destructive way to write around this? Fortunately Delta was only in two to three episodes a week, so the other episode story-lines that didn't involve her could pretty much go on unchanged.

'We decided the best thing to do was for her to suddenly go away, and she was in a relationship at the time . . . so we thought maybe something could happen there to make her do that.'

It was eventually decided that Nina would suddenly fly to India to be with her father, and try to break into Bollywood movies.' Casual writers like Jenni Lewis were brought in as reinforcements.

'I've always been part of the *Neighbours* family. Even when I wasn't on the story team, I was an occasional writer, and I've always been very fond of Ben Michaels who is now the script producer,' Jenni told a *Neighbours* fan site. 'When Delta Goodrem had to suddenly leave the show due to illness, the team found themselves in a bit of a story-lining crisis. They had to re-plot all the stories Delta was involved in, while at the same time keep the current episodes coming. Ben rang and asked if I was available for a couple of months to help out, and I was.'

'There was a heck of a lot of rewrites,' says Ben bluntly.

Nina was written out but kept 'alive' by references to her character. In the wake of the shock of the diagnosis and the sudden disappearance of Delta, the show lost its happy atmosphere. 'It was definitely more subdued for a while,' Stanley remembers. '*Neighbours* is like a big family. Some of the actors and producers have been there for years, and they wouldn't be there if they didn't want to be.'

There was a serious illness in the family, and it took some time before the show was back to normal. The cast and crew got on with work with Delta in their thoughts. 'It was private,' Stanley Walsh says. 'We sent personal letters and flowers, but we didn't intrude.'

Out of respect for Delta's privacy, the cast all refused to be interviewed, and instead Peter Dodds acted as spokesperson for the show. 'We all have our fingers crossed down here in Melbourne and we are looking forward to the day when Delta bounces back into the studio,' he said.

Jay Bunyan (who played one of Delta's love interests on the show) did, however, visit her soon after the diagnosis. 'I went home and saw her and she was good — really good. She's so positive. She knows what she's got to do, and what she's got to get through. She knows all about the treatment and everything that goes along with it. She has a good head on her shoulders, that girl.'

But the cast were deeply affected. When Carla Bonner had a story-line in which she had breast cancer, Carla broke down in tears when she realised she was acting out what Delta was facing in real life. 'I have thought about her every single day,' Carla said.

To the surprise of many, Delta also insisted on shooting the film clip for *Not Me, Not I* as scheduled. Filmed in a secret bush-land location with director Michael Spicca, Delta said firmly, 'I really felt the need to complete the video before I started more treatment.'

She was happy that she was well enough to film the video over two long days. 'She got through it, although it did take a lot out of her,' Wheatley said of the shoot. He described her enthusiasm as simply incredible. 'Nothing was going to stop her filming that video.' Wheatley was amazed. 'It was a brave effort,' he declared.

In September, *Not Me, Not I* debuted at No. 2 and within two weeks of its release went to No. 1. In the wake of the cancer announcement, sales of *Innocent Eyes* went up by 40 per cent, and it was still at No. 1 six months after its release. Delta's fame, already in overdrive, exploded as people surged to know more about the beautiful young singer and soap star facing a deadly illness. Stores sold out of *Innocent Eyes* and had to reorder stock.

'Look, no publicity is bad publicity if you are front-page news,' says a music industry insider, but agreed that it was the most traumatic way possible to raise your profile. New fans were also older than her traditional teen fan base, intrigued by her songs, her beauty and her illness. 'I only vaguely knew about her as a girl on *Neighbours* and a singer,' says a 27-year-old executive who is now an ardent admirer of Delta's. 'Then I read about the cancer and looked at her pictures and realised how hot she was.'

Delta was appalled by rumours she had made up the cancer for publicity. 'I think those rumours came about because she kept doing appearances and made the film clip after the diagnosis, and of course the ARIA appearance,' says one music insider. 'I remember that was when people started asking questions, because they were so surprised that her family didn't completely pull her out of the limelight for several months. I mean, there is of course no truth to the rumours and she is obviously seriously ill, and people were very worried about her . . . but questions were asked.'

Delta recently made thinly veiled comments that it was suggested to her by advisors that she capitalise on her cancer. 'I had some people working with me who talked to me about turning my health issue into a positive thing for my career. I was sitting there trying to get my head around the fact I could die and I was being told that I could somehow use this to my advantage.'

Given she is a cancer sufferer in the public eye, psychologist Professor Phyllis Butow was not surprised Delta kept smiling to her fans, filming and accepting awards despite being so desperately ill. 'She would have felt a responsibility to portray an extraordinary level of coping,' she explains. 'Those in the public eye are expected to be role models, and Delta is a role model to young girls. This may have put extra pressure on her. She would have been aware, I think, that how she behaved would affect not only the public, but other cancer sufferers as well.'

'Delta's treatment was just disgusting,' says Lea. 'What she went through was awful. But she didn't want anyone to see her sick. She didn't want to scare the little kids.'

The massive publicity about her illness and Delta's continuing presence in the public eye did have a life-saving effect on a little boy in Queensland. Tom Ryan's story, which only recently came to light, revealed how the fourteen-year-old diagnosed himself with Hodgkin's after reading about Delta's diagnosis. 'I knew there were a few symptoms Delta had that I had too,' he said. 'I was waking up in the night with pain in my hips and legs and I felt tired all the time. There were lumps that would come and go, and I was pale.'

Although paediatricians declared his symptoms were growing pains, Tom knew instinctively, like Delta, that something was wrong. He was eventually proved right and, although he is now seriously ill because the cancer is at an advanced stage, his mother thinks without Tom reading about Delta, things may have been so much worse.

As Phyllis Butow suggested, Tom looked to Delta for inspiration. 'It's been very hard seeing Tom go through so much, but seeing Delta look so good and so positive has really helped him a lot,' says Tom's mother. 'It must be even harder to go through in the public eye, and for Delta to come out and say "I've had it, but I'm OK" is wonderful for kids like Tom.'

Delta and Tom Ryan recently met in Sydney, on the eve of the ARIAs in 2004. The young man and the star were worlds apart, but cancer is a powerful bond. When Tom asked Delta about her scars, she showed him the lines on her neck and revealed her heartbreak over the loss of her hair. 'At least you've got a boy cut and don't have to grow it long. Mine was blonde and straight, and now it's dark and curly.' Tom, from rural Queensland, said that Delta made him feel special, and Delta was full of praise for the boy. 'He's a beautiful soul,' she said.

Tom knows exactly what his idol endured as she faced her

"I always really loved my hair and it was so much a part of me . . . Finally it was almost all gone except for a little tuft. I had a comb-over at eighteen."

Delta

own cancer treatment. So too did another teenage fan, already fighting cancer, who said she wouldn't wish cancer on her worst enemy. 'I told Delta that it makes you grow up fast, that it's a hard battle, but one that teaches you to love life. You realise it's not what life throws at you, it's how you deal with it,' she says. It was advice Delta would later echo in her own words, as she told of her fight with Hodgkin's disease.

'Cancer is a journey for her. She thinks if she can help one person, then there's a reason for it, and her fame. The boy who was in *New Idea* . . . We have had many stories like that. Kids are getting diagnosed earlier because of Delta,' says Lea.

Exhausted after making the film clip, Delta was forced to take a break from her incredible career to concentrate on the chemotherapy and radiation. Accepting an MTV award (the Australian International Viewers Choice Award) in September, she briefly made a filmed appearance at home with dramatically shortened hair. The head of MTV Australia, Helen Ryan, gave Delta the award at her Glenhaven home. 'Thank you to all my viewers and to all my amazing and dedicated fans,' Delta said.

A friend says that Delta remained positive. 'When she talked about the chemotherapy to me it was like she was taking an aspirin. I wasn't surprised because that is Delta. It was good to see.' But Delta has now admitted how traumatic the treatment was. She has described the chemotherapy as being like poison that 'sucked out her soul'. She recalls that her veins collapsed from the treatment and she had to wear braces to protect her smile.

Delta had always wanted children as soon as her recording career was where she wanted it to be, but now she had to face the possibility the treatment would cause infertility, so it is likely she considered freezing her eggs. 'I've seen days I never want to see again,' Delta says.

The star struggled to come to terms with why this happened to her. She tried to find meaning in the intense highs and lows of her life. Mark Holden wrote on his website, 'Delta said, "Why did this happen to me? I don't drink, I don't smoke . . . I don't even have a boyfriend." She promised that when she got to the other side of her treatment, she was really going to do some living.'

'Searching for meaning is extremely common,' Professor Butow explains, unsurprised by the star's soul-searching questions. 'People try and find meaning in this uncontrollable thing that has happened to them, because reason makes it more understandable.'

As the chemotherapy and cancer took their toll, Delta's self-confidence plummeted as she lost her hair and became bloated with the treatment. The star was a vulnerable, sick and frightened teenager. 'I think it was hard for her to feel she was losing her natural beauty,' says a friend. 'But she knew she had to go through it. She was very focused.'

'I always really loved my hair and it was so much a part of me,' Delta told *The Australian Women's Weekly*. 'I didn't mind that much at the start. I told myself, hair is hair. It grows back. Then it started to fall out more and more and I wasn't prepared for that. There was hair everywhere. The drain was clogged with it after a shower. I'd run my hands through it and clumps would come away in my hands. Finally it was almost all gone except for a little tuft. I had a comb-over at eighteen.'

At the same time as she'd lost all her hair, she won a hairdressing award for celebrity style. But Delta hid her misery and emotions from the others in the oncology ward. 'I've met people who were on the cancer ward with her and they say she was amazingly stoic and an inspiration,' says a friend. 'She brought her teddy bears into the treatment and the poor kid tried to hide her suffering as she absolutely went into the depths.'

'Since this whole cancer thing happened, I've never heard her say, "Why me?" I've never heard her say she felt sorry for herself. She's more concerned about her family and how it's affecting her younger brother,' says friend Molly Meldrum.

In interviews about her cancer fight, Molly said Delta still managed to laugh even in her bleakest moments. When he first saw her soon after the diagnosis, he said she was laughing and crying with the emotional shock of what had happened to her. She managed to find her sense of humour about her hair too.

Molly said that when he met up with Delta and her mother during her cancer treatment, 'Delta was wearing a baseball cap and she was still so beautiful.' She teased Molly and asked if she could borrow his trademark hat for public appearances. 'I told her, unlike her, my hair wouldn't grow back.'

Molly gave her one of his hats for her nineteenth birthday celebration. Former boyfriend Jay Till claimed that he and she had now reunited, and that she attended his birthday party wearing a red wig and seemed in good spirits.

Aware of the trauma many women go through as their looks are ravaged by cancer treatment, family friend Joanne Meehan (NSW state mnager of Look Good . . . Feel Better) immediately offered her help. 'Of course I was very saddened to hear of her cancer. I sent her some get well cards and some brochures and said if she wanted to come to a workshop I would take her, but her mum said it wasn't the right time and thanked me for it,' Joanne says.

Joanne says teenagers battling cancer are deeply affected by the loss of their hair, loss of eyelashes and even eyebrows. 'It's difficult at any age and especially when you are young,' Joanne says. 'A lot don't want to leave the house, they feel awkward. And I can imagine with the whole nation watching and to have no privacy when you are ill, all those feelings are exacerbated . . . But I think she was comforted by the thousands of well-wishers.'

Delta says she was inundated with cards, gifts and messages from fans and concerned Australians. Her website received over 40,000 messages of support, and magazines like *TV Hits* and *Total Girl* were swamped with worried fans sending their love to Delta.

Just as she had been overwhelmed by her fans at her signings, now Delta was overcome with the outpouring of love streaming to her house, to her music company and to *Neighbours*. 'We knew how popular she is, not just for her work on *Neighbours*, but also for her music — but no one could remember a reaction like this,' Stanley Walsh says of the massive response.

Delta was so grateful and humbled by these demonstrations of love. She was determined to appear at the ARIA Awards and show her fans she was doing well.

Lea was grimly determined too. 'Delta will get her dream,' she said on the eve of the Awards. 'She will have her big night.' With ten award nominations, the public build-up to her appearance was huge. Delta deliberately instructed doctors to stop her treatment so she could be well enough to attend. She explained that going to this glittering occasion was like a light at the end of the tunnel for her — a reward for the gruelling regime of chemotherapy and radiation she was enduring.

She thought about attending the Awards with her bare head exposed but, ever conscious of being a role model and worried that she would upset her young fans with such a dramatic and stark appearance, she instead wore a wig made out of her own hair, and a soft pink gown by designer Lisa Ho. 'I wanted to feel feminine that night, and to relax,' Delta says.

While Delta was inundated with offers to be dressed by major fashion houses such as Gucci, Chanel, Calvin Klein, Armani and Collette Dinnigan, who had dressed her for the 2002 Logies, at the last minute Delta rang Lisa, asking that she make her something beautiful. Her only request was that it be pink.

Delta said she was feeling excited and overwhelmed by the attention and build-up. 'I feel very nervous but I'm happy to be here . . . it feels so special.'

She looked frail but exquisite when she appeared surrounded by her beaming family. Her days of attending awards functions in anonymity, while other stars shone around her, were now well and truly behind her. This night, where she'd walked so many times in her dreams, was now glittering before her. A passionate high, a passionate low.

That night, Delta made record history, winning seven ARIAs: Best Female Artist, Best New Artist-Album, Best New Artist-Single, Best Pop Release, Single of the Year, Highest Selling Album and Highest Selling Single. Delta also took home a further two 'unofficial' awards presented on the night: The Channel [V] Oz Artist of the Year award and the *Video Hits* Music Video of the Year award. 'God it's boring when one artist scoops, but Delta deserved it,' said a music insider admiringly.

'I'm really speechless,' Delta said of her record-breaking number of awards. 'I can't put words to it. Every year you dream of winning, and when you finally do it's amazing.'

She broke down in tears when Savage Garden singer Darren Hayes sang *Lost Without You*. Her voice was still not strong enough to perform that night, and the emotion of winning, the outpouring of love for her, and the longing to sing, finally overcame her. 'I thought I was doing really well, keeping composed. But as soon as he started singing, I lost it.'

Speaking of her frustration at not being able to sing during her treatment, Delta said at the ARIAs, 'I look at everyone up there and I can't wait to get back into it. I would love to get back up there, but you have to look after yourself.'

She took the opportunity to thank all those who had helped her, including a much-discussed brief thankyou to Glenn Wheatley, and then won more hearts by her emotional thankyou to her fans. 'To all the Australian public out there, if you ever think there's not wonderful people out there in the world, then come and visit my house and see all the beautiful letters and well-wishes that I got in the last two months, because there are really beautiful people out there.'

But there was controversy, as well as rumours of romance on the night. Network Ten publicist, Steve Murphy, introduced *Australian Idol* winner Guy Sebastian to his idol. A picture of Delta was on his mobile phone, and the young and incredibly talented born-again Christian adored the clean-living, beautiful singer. 'There was some chaste kissing and cuddling,' a source claimed to a music gossip site.

'When recording his album, Guy Sebastian dedicated the song

My Beautiful Friend to Delta,' says a music insider. According to gossip, they formed a close friendship until Delta fell for Mark Philippoussis. 'Guy's not the most experienced guy with girls,' says a friend of his. 'I think it woke him up a bit.'

Another besotted fan on the night was Jon Coghill, the drummer of ARIA-award-winning band Powderfinger, who teased her with notes all night saying, 'Bet you can't win Best Male Artist.'

The extraordinary response to Delta at the ARIAs overwhelmed her. 'I'm so thankful that the Australian people have connected with my music the way that they have. Thank you from the bottom of my heart and I look forward to seeing you all soon.'

She later added that she now felt particularly connected to fans — and others — with cancer. 'People have really reached out and touched me. I've always done charity work, but before I used to feel awkward when I met sick children. I never quite connected. Now I know what they're going through, I understand their fears and their hopes — because they are mine.'

The night of the ARIA awards was like a dream for Delta. The accolades were proof that some dreams come true but, like Cinderella, Delta had to return to the depths before she could take her place in the spotlight once more and enjoy a happy ending.

The awards night boosted her spirits before she returned to more treatment and radiation. Her body was shielded to protect her as much as possible from the ill-effects of radiation, but her smile, her voice, and her very life were still threatened.

After four months of intensive treatment (from July to October), Delta had also formed a close friendship with Trish Chronopoulos, who is the nurse unit manager at St Vincent's

Hospital's oncology outpatients clinic. Delta thanked Trish and Trish's colleagues at St Vincent's at the ARIAs and describes Trish as an 'unbelievable little angel'.

Trish returns the praise, saying that Delta — one of 800 patients she sees a month — is an 'amazing person to know. A real role model. She has so much wisdom for her age. She's so great to be around.' Lest anyone think she was starstruck, Trish adds, 'It's great meeting famous people but once you get to know them, they're like anybody else.'

Delta celebrated her nineteenth birthday and her awards quietly at her home with family and friends, reflecting on her life and amazing achievement. 'She wore a cap over her head and looked so sick and frail,' says Helen Wilson, wife of Network Ten newsreader Ron Wilson. 'But she smiled and faced everyone and her personality really shone through the sickness that night. I don't know if many people could have done that. I felt quite emotional watching her.'

For the girl who hated to sit still, resting from the ordeal of chemotherapy and radiotherapy was a challenge in itself. 'With Delta, the challenge is getting her to stop working,' says Lea. 'I'm so proud of her work ethic, but she has had to learn to relax and rest because of her health.' The sudden feeling of having nothing to do but retreat and rest was a huge shock after a year in which she had achieved the No. 1 hit single and album in Australia.

Delta, someone who always feels passionate about life, described the year of her cancer and recovery as 'bipolar'. Peter Dodds, executive producer of *Neighbours*, correctly warned that Delta would find it hard doing nothing as she came out the other side of her treatment.

'Recovering, she was bored,' agrees a friend. 'She wanted to be well enough to do things. She got frustrated because she didn't have the normal life and energy levels, and found it strange to find all these people knocking on her door who she hadn't seen for years.'

To cope, Delta retreated to her peace: her song writing. Delta has now revealed that some of the songs she wrote were so angry that she will never record or perform them. Others, like *Extraordinary Day*, are still intensely personal compositions but she feels they are appropriate to include on her follow-up album.

Delta missed singing terribly. Used to bursting into song at any opportunity, the anxiety she felt about her voice weighed on her deeply and, for the first time, she felt depression. While experiencing depression is common among cancer patients, for Delta it was a dark episode in her life.

'It drove me nuts, absolutely crazy,' she says. 'Sitting there not being able to sing . . . it's like an athlete who has been out for a year and suddenly they have to get back to match-fit form. I'd never felt depression. You're talking to someone who'd bounce into a room. I'd never felt as low as I got, never ever. I'd be lying if I said I was always positive. I remember thinking, What is going on here? I'm eighteen. But not for one second did I think, Oh no. It was more like, so this is my next challenge, this is the next chapter of my life.'

'Depression is common following the cancer diagnosis and treatment,' says psychologist Melanie Price. 'It's an additional burden.'

Vince Pizzinga and Delta discussed when she could begin recording her next album, but her voice was still delicate and

Delta had to wait it out until her health and vocal chords could withstand the workload. Vince consoled her, and Delta took heart from his listening to her vision for the next album. Vince knew it would be much more sophisticated because of Delta's dramatic life experiences.

'We have had a lot of conversations, not just about music, all sorts of things, and she is itching to get back into it. She is heart-broken she is not in the studio working,' Vince said at the time. 'But it's a case of getting better first. The priority for her is to rest and recuperate. She's gone through a pretty traumatic experience and is still going through it. I'm not sure people appreciate how traumatic it has been for her.'

At Christmas, Delta released *Predictable*, the fifth single from *Innocent Eyes*. Without her doing any publicity, the song shot to No. 2, and was only prevented from being No. 1 on debut because of her friend Guy Sebastian's *Idol* hit, *When Angels Brought Me Here*. Predictably, it then went to No. 1.

The single also contained a version of Beatle John Lennon's *Happy Xmas (War is Over)*, which was recorded just after she was diagnosed with Hodgkin's and once she'd obtained permission from Lennon's widow, Yoko Ono. This song was also included on a Christmas CD released by various artists to raise money for the Salvation Army. No doubt, Delta longed for a Happy Xmas too.

Announcing she'd finished treatment, she told fans she was trying to get out a little more and enjoy herself. On 21 December, Delta posted her Christmas message on her website. 'Well the last few months have been an interesting journey. There has been a lot of discussion about why I haven't been on the forum. I can safely say it has nothing to do with my wonderful friends here. That it is completely to do with the fact I have been sick. I have finished my treatment . . . only four more sleeps to go until Christmas. I think my brother Trent has bought me a Harry Potter calendar, which I'm excited about.'

She also took the opportunity to chide those who had been negative on her forum. If Delta hadn't been a singer, she would have been a motivational speaker and author. 'This is a positive forum. Where we stay positive and have goals, dreams, aspirations, make friends and have a good old chat because it should be fun . . .'

She didn't know that just around the corner was her own Christmas wish — for a romance that would come from out of the blue.

"She's even more beautiful on the inside. And that's what I fell in love with."

Mark Philippoussis

CHAPTER 9
Out of the Blue

It was always going to be front-page news. Delta Goodrem, a baseball cap over her bald head and shading her frail face, sat down court-side at Sydney's Adidas International to watch tennis star Mark Philippoussis play.

With the divorce of Nicole and Tom, Australia needed another 'super couple' to admire, and the most surprising pairing of the year sent editors into story heaven. 'He's game, she's set — is it a match?' asked one cheeky headline. To those who know Delta and Mark, the match was on from the first meeting. 'They were besotted with each other, both of them, right from the start,' declared a friend.

When he first heard of the relationship with Mark, Ron Wilson was not surprised, and commented, 'She's into the whole sports scene and there is no question she is a sports fan. And she's mature for her age, so I don't think the age difference is a problem.'

The romance began as Mark and a friend were browsing through a Melbourne record store. He picked up the *Innocent Eyes* CD and admired the girl with long hair and a beautiful smile shining on the cover. His friend explained that the artist, Delta, was having treatment for Hodgkin's disease, just like Mark's father, who has had the illness three times.

Mark sent Delta flowers and a card, but Delta says she did not receive the flowers as she was in Sydney and they were sent to her Melbourne management. She did, however, receive the card, and the well-mannered girl began her long list of thankyous in December when she felt well enough.

She says in *The Australian Women's Weekly* article, 'I called him, we had a little chat and then a little while later, he called back and asked me to the tennis.' She was feeling very vulnerable. Never confident about her looks, she felt self-conscious about the loss of her crowning glory — her long, feminine hair. But she had told herself it was now time to start living, instead of simply working.

'Cancer is a way of reassessing priorities,' says psychologist Melanie Price. 'People work out what is worth putting time into, and what is not. You put your own health into perspective and go with things that are important.'

Delta was coming out of a traumatic experience. She needed the freedom to be able to do what felt right to her and to take opportunities. Says Melanie Price, 'People who have had cancer become a lot stronger about saying no.' And yes. She accepted his invitation and went to the tennis with Trent and her friend Lalitha Svendra.

In the days following the tennis, Delta and Mark lunched together in Bronte, and at the glamorous beach restaurant Hugo's in Bondi Beach. The couple wore matching caps and Mark was photographed gazing at Delta with an adoring smile. Delta looked frail as she peered up at him, but there was a connection obvious to all who observed them. Still, protective of her privacy, Sony firmly announced, 'Delta and Mark are just good friends.'

This interlude was a beautiful distraction for Delta as her gruelling treatment neared completion and her cancer check-up tests loomed. When she suddenly appeared at the Australian Open in Melbourne with friends Molly Meldrum and Nick Giannopoulos, Delta explained demurely that she came down on the spur of the moment to get some fresh air. 'It was a last-minute decision. Let's do it — you only live once.'

Lea came with her as chaperone, and mother and daughter stayed at the Crown Promenade, while Mark stayed at the Crown

"Mark is a very caring young man. And he came along at just the right time for Delta. Whoever was sprinkling fairy dust around at that time I thank them, because Mark has made such a difference."

Lea Goodrem

Delta with Mark Philippoussis in Bondi

Delta with Mark Philippoussis at the 2004 Logies

Towers. A murmur swept through the crowd as she took her seat at the Rod Laver Arena in Mark's reserved box. The crowd watched delightedly when Mark misfired into the net, then glanced up at Delta and shrugged affectionately. Delta giggled next to her mother.

Delta also took Mark as her date to a five-star dinner in St Kilda and, when cheekily asked by a fan if he was 'born to try', Mark replied, 'Not me, not I.'

Psychologist and popular culture commentator, Karen Brooks, is not surprised that Mark and Delta found each other so publicly, or that their celebrity love match was so popular with their fans. 'It is quite usual for celebrities of the calibre of Mark and Delta to seek each other out. Like many demanding professions, it's really only someone else in the industry who can relate to, and empathise with, the demands placed on you.

'As a celebrity, there is a real sense that you are a public property. The public feel they know you, and that they have the right to comment and judge you on the basis of what the media has chosen to portray. Mark has both suffered and benefited from this in the past. He is depicted as strong, but also fiery. Delta on the other hand has been constructed like a fairytale princess — she is the beauty to his handsome beast. He appears protective of her, but he will also give her permission to be strong.'

'I think they are good for each other, and I hope they are in love,' said a friend at this time. 'I think being in an independent, mature relationship with a man who has experience and independence under his belt is great for her.'

Mark, while unwilling to give too much away during these heady early days, said in a press conference that 'Delta was an extremely strong girl going through what she has.' But the romantic mood turned ugly when Mark suddenly bombed out of the Open to a Moroccan tennis player, Hicham Azari, who was ranked 51. When a child in the crowd burst into tears during the match, Mark said, 'I know how you feel.'

Delta needed a hug and a kiss from Molly Meldrum to cope with the tension and Mark's growing frustration as he lost in straight sets. As disappointed as everyone else by his performance, Mark said, 'I felt pretty confident going into the match. To be honest, I didn't feel any pressure. Azari played, I thought, a flawless match. I tried to do everything out there . . . And I just . . . I sort of let 'em down.'

Pat Cash, Mark's former tennis coach, told media he was unimpressed with Mark's performance. 'It looked like Mark was up all night, doing whatever,' he said. Mark, horrified because this comment embarrassed Delta and was offensive to him, rang Cash and abused and threatened him on the phone, to the point where Cash said he was going to get a restraining order. 'I have never been spoken to like that, ever,' Cash said. 'I'm a straight shooter . . . I get paid to tell it how I see it.'

It wasn't the first time Cash had spoken bluntly about Mark being easily distracted. In his published autobiography, Cash wrote that Mark visited strip clubs on the eve of big tournaments, and that he had had to persuade Mark not to spend the night with Anna Kournikova on the eve of grand slam matches.

'Pat didn't even know Mark was going out with Delta,' claims a friend of Cash's. 'Mark has a huge reputation on the circuit for partying — that's where that comment came from. It had nothing to do with her.'

Still, the damage was done, and with two tennis stars fighting over a beautiful singer, the story was too good to fade away. 'I was just feeling good about myself and about Mark, and then it was splashed all over the papers . . .' Delta said. 'For Pat to put a really bad slant on something that was lovely, something that came out of nowhere and wonderful . . . it was disrespectful.'

The controversy was too much for Delta and she brought forward her holiday to Los Angeles to get some peace. She craved an escape. She wanted to be able to go out of the house and not fret about which hat to wear — she wanted to be herself. Ironically, the place Delta chose to disappear was the country where she most longed to be No. 1: the US. She did get some respite but, being Delta, it was impossible to disappear. Asked about Mark at the Grammy Awards after-party in LA, Delta teased, 'Is Mark back here? Oh, goodness!'

Normally based in Florida and San Diego, Mark needed to breathe too after the emotions of meeting Delta and the fallout from the Australian Open. His confrontation with Cash — with whom he was already on tense terms — created a rift so deep that there was little chance of the two tennis greats ever repairing it. He wore a Greek letter 'delta' at the Davis Cup match in Adelaide, and then abruptly left the country to be with the singer and her mother in LA.

'January was a tough month for me,' Mark said. 'Pretty hectic and frustrating. I love Australia. I love my country so much and these things happen and that makes you want to get away. And that's frustrating, because I'm already away 85 per cent of the year. And it's such a long year . . . It's no good feeling drained, when the year has just started.

'When you are put under a microscope like that, 24/7, on and off the court, it's very tough. For a split second I wanted to get out of the game, but then I woke up and came to my senses.'

Mark later admitted the fallout with Cash nearly reduced him to tears. 'He's a pretty nervous guy,' says Peter McNamara. 'Emotionally it affected him and pushed him into his shell. His tennis has been affected because he just doesn't seem to have his heart and soul in it.'

Cash's comments emphasised his playboy past, and Mark would have been all too aware of his party-boy image scaring his beautiful, sheltered girlfriend away. Since bursting onto the circuit with his fearsome 200-kilometre-an-hour serve, 'The Scud' had become known as a wild boy who, a tennis insider says, is 'not great with money'. An observer who saw him at a celebrity golf tournament in Queensland in his early days laughed as he remembers Mark striding around the golf course with a gorgeous girl on each arm.

But friends insisted he was far more complex and sensitive than his party-boy image suggested. They admitted that he liked to be associated with well-known, glamorous women; Anna Kournikova, French actress Melanie Maudran, Sarah Michelle Gellar and Tara Reid are all ex-girlfriends or dates. But he split with Tara a few months before meeting Delta, reportedly because he found Tara was unable to cope with the demands the tennis circuit made on his time.

His serious relationship with Delta seemed to indicate that he was taking a new approach to life, which included moving away from his flashy Florida lifestyle to train with an ex-Navy marine in San Diego. He now seemed to prefer cafes, surfing and watching videos to partying hard. 'He's not the playboy everybody believes him to be,' a friend claimed after the Cash fallout. 'Mark's a really nice, quiet, shy bloke, and it's been great for Delta to have somebody like him around while she recuperates.'

"He's not the playboy everybody believes him to be. Mark's a really **nice, quiet, shy bloke**, and it's been great for Delta to have **somebody like him around** while she recuperates."

A friend

'I come across as a little intimidating at first,' Mark said, commenting on his image. 'A big guy doesn't look so sensitive. If I walk into a place and I've got my head down, people think it's arrogance. But I'm a nice guy. I'm just a young guy trying to live my life. Growing up I have been hurt, and I try to protect myself.

'Everyone matures in different stages. I mean, being a young guy, being a single guy, who all of a sudden gets some fame and money, what are you going to do? Are you going to buy a little town house and train your arse off? Or maybe buy a big house, nice car and party? It's the normal thing to do and I was living, you know, other guys' dreams and then you get it out of your system.'

With Delta, at first he was the model boyfriend. He was extremely respectful — not only of her age, achievements and talent, but also of her battle with Hodgkin's disease, because he'd seen his father suffer so much. It was another connection to bond the two as they spent more time together. He said that he'd fallen in love with Delta because of her 'courage, tenacity and selflessness'. And that he was proud to be the boyfriend of Australia's golden girl.

'She's even more beautiful on the inside,' Philippoussis told interviewers, in a departure from his usual line on privacy. 'And that's what I fell in love with.'

While unwilling to discuss Delta's private life, her theatrical agent, Stephen Harmon, is not surprised that Mark fell for Delta. 'She has this aura, this sweetness, that everyone falls in love with,' he says affectionately.

Tennis insiders at this time speculated that Mark was a different person to the one who had first burst onto the tennis circuit. He showed every sign of being head over heels in love with Delta. 'He's a changed man, that's for sure. Mark was quite the skirt chaser, but he's shelved all that for Delta,' said a tennis insider. 'He used to have eyes for every cute girl he met, but now he seems to love only Delta. Ever since he's been with her, he's changed dramatically. His wild party-boy image has gone. A lot of folks are saying she's done the impossible — she's tamed Mark.' Time would tell for how long . . .

In LA, Mark stayed close to Delta. He met her at her glamorous Sunset Marquis Hotel, just off Sunset Boulevard, and slept off his jet lag in her room. But, protective of her daughter's health and heart, Lea chaperoned Delta and Mark to a Sting concert. When asked by reporters what she thought of the tennis player, Lea declared that he was a 'lovely boy' who was very supportive of Delta.

Lea encouraged the relationship, believing it to be good for her daughter. She told the *Weekly*, 'Mark is a very caring young man. And he came along at just the right time for Delta. Whoever was sprinkling fairy dust around at that time I thank them, because Mark has made such a difference. He came into her life when she was at her lowest ebb and she wasn't feeling physically attractive. There wasn't a lot of hair under that cap, and he didn't see any of it. He didn't even notice it. He made her take her hat off all the time. She would wear wigs and he would ask her what she was doing.'

Delta confessed to a friend that Mark made her '*sooo* happy' and that 'she was crazy about him'. Mark surfed and trained at his Californian home while Delta shopped and met with industry producers. She also brought her keyboard with her to write songs. Designer Lisa Ho, who met up with Delta in LA, said her keyboard was the first thing Delta set up when she entered her hotel room.

Mark and Delta held hands as they walked, and kissed as they waited to cross the street. The romance of the night they went to the Sting concert was capped off with a backstage meeting with the singer, where Delta said she had a spiritual conversation with him.

Delta, her head uncovered for the first time to reveal rich brown hair, kissed Mark as they sat at a Santa Monica cafe and window-shopped at a jewellery store, Chopard. These were happy days under a blue Californian sky, with the future unfolding before her.

To Delta, after the exhaustion of her diagnosis and treatment and huge success, these blissful days in LA almost allowed her to forget her sickness and her celebrity. But her ill-health was still beneath the surface of her happiness and always ready to throw her into turmoil.

Just before flying home to Australia, still delicate after months of chemotherapy and radiotherapy and with her immune system weak, Delta caught a cold. She spiked a high fever and deteriorated. Her worried mother rushed her to hospital, where she was treated with antibiotics as a precaution.

Frustrated at this setback, Delta still kept her spirits up amid rumours she'd secretly booked into the hospital for more chemotherapy. A friend denied it was for treatment saying, reasonably, if she needed more cancer treatment, she would have it at home.

But after her healing holiday with Mark and her mother, she quickly picked up again and recovered from the scare. 'She looked fantastic,' says a friend who was with her in LA. 'You'd never know she'd just been in hospital, and Mark was a great support to her.' Delta recovered with her mum and Mark by her side.

Before leaving the US, Mark and Delta flew to Mark's home in Del Ray, Florida, to meet his father Nick. Like Lea, Nick has been a huge force in guiding Mark's tennis career as his son's coach. 'Nick knows where his son is at, and what his son needs,' tennis perennial Wally Masur said of the father and son's close relationship. 'You have a chat with Nick and he explains what's going on and you say, "You know what? I think you're right." '

Nick is nothing if not a survivor, having beaten Hodgkin's three times. During the relaxing days of privacy and romance at Mark's Florida home, Nick inspired Delta with his determination to live. Surrounded by Mark and Nick's five pet Pomeranian dogs, Delta and the older man spoke intently about the emotions of their diagnosis and treatment. His survival from relapses was a powerful reminder of how the fighting spirit can conquer cancer, but also of how Delta could never feel free of this disease.

'The fear of the cancer returning is the biggest fear,' says Melanie Price. But, always positive, Delta was determined to concentrate on living her life. As she always said, if it was worth doing, it was worth doing well . . . for however long or short her life was going to be.

She had youth, family and love . . . but Delta was soon to learn that, like life, love was never guaranteed.

"It is Delta's dream, not my dream. I'm a shy person and I don't like to be in the papers, and maybe that's why some people think I am harsh."

Lea Goodrem

CHAPTER 10

Lea and Delta

As her daughter strode to stardom, Lea was there, holding her hand and encouraging her to reach for her dreams. Now Lea was faced with her biggest challenge: nursing Delta through cancer.

Delta said that, as soon as she was told of the cancer, she wanted her mother. 'As long as I could smell her hair, and know she was near, I felt protected.'

The night of the announcement, Lea seemed as strong as ever. Visibly shaken, but still polite and open, Denis Goodrem told the growing press pack that he wanted to wait until Lea came home before making any statement.

Music columnist Christine Sams remembers that as soon as Lea came home from St Vincent's Hospital, where Delta had been seeing doctors, 'the mood changed considerably'. Father and daughter were shielded from the press and Lea was at the front line. When Christine rang the 'delta.com' doorbell one more time, she faced Lea.

But while she tried to remain polite and business-like, Lea, according to Christine's account in *Sunday Life* magazine, was visibly exhausted and sagging. 'Delta's mother was struggling to maintain her stoicism and, without thinking, I stretched my hand towards her shoulder as though to comfort her. At the slightest touch, Lea fell forward and clung to me for a few seconds like her knees had been about to buckle.' The spontaneous gesture of comfort revealed how much Lea was suffering too.

'I think Lea's health has been affected by Delta's treatment,' says Ron Wilson. 'I think she needed a good lie down more than Delta did.'

Lea has revealed her own agony at Delta's cancer diagnosis in the *Women's Weekly* exclusive. She was by Delta's side as they spent hours with doctors explaining the results, the disease and the fact that, because they had found multiple tumours around Delta's throat, she needed an emergency operation. The operation was so urgent it was scheduled for the next morning.

Lea recalled that during the eternity of waiting for the operation, she had managed to keep her composure. 'Until that moment, I had held up pretty well. I was trying to be strong for Delta. I was just doing what needed to be done, so Delta wouldn't worry. But while we were waiting to go into the operating theatre, I lost it. You can't imagine what it was like to be sending your daughter into surgery, not knowing what is going to happen.'

Professor Butow says that carers of those with cancer suffer silently and mothers feel the pain most of all. 'It is not natural for a parent to be facing the potential death of a child and it's the hardest of all emotions to go through. The most common emotions in facing the loss of the child are a feeling of loss of control and not knowing how to help. The illness puts the family into turmoil.'

'It's very common to blame yourself, and I would be surprised if Lea didn't experience this,' says a father who has lost a daughter to cancer. 'You think, Was it something I did? Did I put too much pressure on her?'

'Words cannot describe it,' Lea says of her emotional reaction to her daughter's life-threatening illness. 'It's overwhelming. We have had friends who lost children in car accidents, who had the police knock at their doors and have their lives destroyed. But at least with the diagnosis, there is a chance. You have to hope and pray . . . but there is a chance. There is life.'

Knowing her mother was suffering, Delta reached out to the

"I am incredibly proud of my daughter, not because of how many pop records she has sold but because of how she's handling what she is going through."

Lea Goodrem

woman who meant most to her in the world. 'I looked at Mum and something just kicked in. I knew it was my turn to be the strong one, to help her get through. I kept telling them everything would be OK.'

After the three-hour operation, her mother was with her as yet more tumours were found around Delta's throat. 'With cancer — I haven't been through it myself, fortunately — but as a mother, it must be an ordeal,' Joanne Meehan reflects. 'You can't control what is going to happen; you have to put your daughter in the hands of medical professionals . . . It must be a terrible feeling of insecurity.'

The intense period of Delta's stardom and cancer diagnosis has brought the mother and daughter even closer together. For Lea, the cancer ordeal has shown her daughter's strength, which she always knew was there.

'I am incredibly proud of my daughter, not because of how many pop records she has sold but because of how she's handling what she is going through,' Lea said in the months after the diagnosis. 'Singing is all Delta wanted to do. Ever. But since she started this fight, she has been absolutely amazing.' Lea said later that, while she hoped Delta would win the ARIAs, what she most wanted for her was her return to good health.

The closeness between Lea and Delta is remarked upon by all who know them, and even those who don't know the family are struck by the mother and daughter's connection. 'She is the force in Delta's life, you can just tell,' says a fan who follows Delta's life in the press.

When asked who was her best friend and role model, Delta simply replied, 'My mum'. 'She puts up with a lot. She goes through everything with me. We're like best friends and I love and respect her so much.'

Since recognising Delta's talent and determination as a child, Lea has supported and fostered her creativity. She and Denis were determined to give their children an environment where they could thrive and dream; Lea said it was the perfect place to encourage individual thoughts and personality.

She also never ridiculed or trivialised her daughter when she said she wanted to be a singer, and Delta is grateful that her mother took her dream so seriously and got behind her. 'We never said you can't become something. If you say you want to be a singer, then fine, go and be a singer,' Lea said of her support. She told her daughter to put her heart into it, and do it well.

This environment, thinks astrologer Karen Moregold, helped the natural force of Delta's personality blossom early. 'While star characteristics are present from the time of birth, it depends on the environment surrounding them as to when they develop,' Karen says. 'The characteristics really peak in the teenage years, as you can see with Delta.'

Her mother's love and support for her led Delta to dedicate one of her biggest hits to her family. 'I wrote *Innocent Eyes* with Vince Pizzinga. I was rehearsing a performance of *Born To Try* and I looked up to see Mum crying. I said, "Mum, what's wrong?" And she said, "I'm just so proud of you." Then I was performing in front of thousands and I looked out to see that Mum was still there. She's always there for me. This is a song for my family.'

'Often they would talk about the early days of Delta performing and cry and laugh,' says a friend. 'It's a goal they had together since Delta was a child, and I have truly never seen a closer mother and daughter.'

Stanley Walsh was struck by the closeness of the mother-and-daughter team when Delta and her mum moved to Melbourne. 'They are very close, incredibly so,' he says. 'I thought she was really nice,' says Rick Maier. 'She didn't strike me as a stage mum at all.'

Delta was so grateful her mother was with her as her career exploded. Only eighteen, Delta turned to her mother for support and honesty as her world became a very public place. Lea would often be with Delta at her appearances, quietly shedding tears of pride over her daughter's God-given talent and the success they had achieved together.

Lea took Delta's talent and determination as a sign she was meant to do something special. 'The Goodrems are a good Christian family,' says the friend. 'She and her mother both wear crucifixes and Lea often said, "God is watching over you, Delta," when Delta was about to sing.'

Despite her daughter's incredible achievements, Lea would still find herself telling her pop-star daughter to tidy up her messy room or that she didn't look great in an outfit or, if Delta wanted constructive criticism, advising her how her performance could have been better. 'Nobody could get a big head in our house,' Delta said once, grateful for her mother's honesty.

To Delta and close friends, Lea is a positive influence in a tough, very competitive industry. 'She gives Delta good advice. She is her guiding light,' says Joanne Meehan loyally. 'Since Delta has been in the limelight, that family has been through madness and mayhem. Her mother has tremendous love for her and is absolutely an amazing lady. She is so very supportive of Delta and they are especially close, I think, because of Delta's singing career and what they have been through together.'

American author Fran Lebowitz defined a stage mum as 'a female parent, who, to put it kindly, has taken it upon herself to instil in her child theatrical ambition and success. The entire upbringing of the child has as its goal that basis.'

Lea is aware she is regarded as a stage mother by many in the industry, but she insists that she is not musical and Delta's incredible talent is not a family trait, nor is she interested in the spotlight. Her intense involvement comes from protection and love and supporting her daughter's dream, rather than a want or need for publicity, and Delta wanted her there by her side. 'People don't know how hard she works but she makes her own decisions, and Delta's her own person,' Lea declares. She added, 'It is Delta's dream, not my dream. I'm a shy person and I don't like to be in the papers, and maybe that's why some people think I am harsh.'

It may have been Delta's dream, but Lea's support has been extraordinary. 'Lea treats things very seriously,' reflects Ron Wilson. 'When you take her on, you're taking the bull by the horns, and it is her way or not at all. I've known the family since Delta was in nappies — and without question, without Lea, Delta wouldn't be known as well as she is now. You need dedicated backing to get there.'

'Professionally and personally, nothing ever happened without Lea being 100 per cent involved,' says a music source. 'At first I wasn't surprised because Delta was so young, but as she got older it became more pronounced.'

Like Anna Kournikova's mother, who is heavily involved in her daughter's tennis career, Lea has made sacrifices for her daughter. Kournikova recalled that her mother sold the family TV to buy her first tennis racquet. Unwilling to let her teenage daughter live

“She’s the only one at the end of the day that has got my interests 100 per cent at heart. I love her — and I hope one day that I will be as strong as her.”

Delta

alone in Melbourne without support, Lea lived apart from her husband and son to be with her.

Lea accompanied Delta on her frequent international trips, spending more time away from Denis and Trent, and only rushing back to Sydney to see them when Delta was filming *Neighbours*. She has been in the US with Delta as they attempt to crack the US market. 'She moved from her other child and husband to be with Delta,' says a friend.

The Goodrems' marriage is still together, and Lea dashed home often to see her husband and son. 'They work so hard,' says Ron Wilson. 'I think it would put tremendous strain on the family. But they still live together; they still live in a suburban home and used to be in the phone book.'

Delta herself said she was amazed and so grateful for her mother's sacrifices for her career, and that she is the only one she could truly trust in her new life. 'I'm very, very close to my mum. My whole family is pretty close and you really have to be. I need Mum, just for the fact that I will walk off stage and people will say I was good and I can ask Mum to tell me the truth. She'll always be blatantly honest with me. She'll tell me that I was all right, but that she's seen me do better, or tell me straight that I was rubbish. She's the only one at the end of the day that has got my interests 100 per cent at heart. I love her — and I hope one day that I will be as strong as her.'

A source close to the family remarked that this intense protectiveness is known throughout the community. Friends are extremely loyal to the Goodrems and 'report back' about anything Delta-related to Lea.

'Delta is as tough as a mallee bull,' Glenn Wheatley remarked once. 'And Lea is as determined as her daughter.' Alone they are strong individuals, but together they are an amazing force of will.

While Wheatley was once the beacon guiding this determined duo to the promised land of stardom, Lea and Delta are now lighting their own path. In October 2003, just before her much-anticipated appearance at the ARIA Awards in the middle of cancer treatment, Delta announced that she would not be renewing her manager's contract, shocking the music industry and sparking debate over whether this was Delta's or Lea's decision.

Lea was believed to be particularly upset by what she perceived as Wheatley giving higher priority to John Farnham over her daughter and by his attitude to Delta upon his return to Australia from America after she had been diagnosed with cancer. 'Lea was so angry that Wheatley didn't make his first stop the hospital,' a source told newspapers at the time of the split. 'She felt it spoke volumes about what he thought of Delta. After that, the relationship was doomed.'

At the time a source claimed to newspapers that Lea and Delta fired Wheatley following a 'blazing row' after he had been given six months to 'pull his socks up'. Delta hadn't spoken to Wheatley at all in the weeks before the split was announced and the relationship had been deteriorating since before Delta was diagnosed with Hodgkin's disease. 'The past year had been wonderful, but Delta was alone,' this source says of the months before her diagnosis. 'She was working on *Neighbours* all day, then doing her music at night . . .'

Another insider argued that Wheatley had become embroiled in a three-way power struggle with Sony Music and Lea for the young teenage star and was eventually frozen out. 'Wheatley thinks Lea is a dragon lady . . . but really she is protecting her best asset, her daughter,' says a source. 'It's from her heart . . . She is a very, very strong woman.'

Delta says that it was she who ended the relationship with Wheatley, and her mother supported her, rather than her mother telling her what to do. 'It was an easy decision — my relationship with him had not been good for some time,' Delta explained.

She made a special effort to explain her decision to fans via her website when the controversy exploded into the public arena: 'Here is a statement regarding my management,' Delta wrote. 'I am grateful for the work that Glenn has put into my career. However there have been life-changing experiences for me and my wishes are that while I spend time to concentrate on my recovery, I have the time to reassess my life and how I see my future . . .'

And while most believe Lea was behind sacking Wheatley, Phyllis Butow is not surprised Delta chose to end a management in the wake of cancer. 'Cancer is often thought of as an opportunity — not just a cost,' she observes. 'It's an opportunity to think about what is important in life . . . I don't know the statistics but people often make decisions about keeping positive people in their lives and getting out of relationships that they think are negative.'

Wheatley likened the split to a 'divorce' and said he feared it would put further pressure on her health. While gracious in public, behind the scenes he was hurt and furious, particularly towards Lea. 'Poor Glenn thought everything was OK,' says a friend. 'He had no idea what the family thought of him.'

Ron Wilson, who also knows Glenn, talked to the manager in the wake of the split. 'He was distraught. Not in tears, but when a bloke starts hugging you and telling you his woes, you know he's taken it hard. The problem with Glenn and Lea is it became a clash of cultures. Lea can see the endgame, whereas Glenn knew there was a system of doing things.'

'Do you want my honest opinion?' asks a music industry insider. 'Wheatley should have paid more attention to her. He was so engrossed in the Farnham tour and she was promoting all over the place. Her mum and Delta obviously wanted more input.'

With the establishment of Goodrem Management, Lea has now joined the club known as 'momanagers' — a mother guiding their celebrity child in sport or music. It's a more positive term than stage mother, which implies the mum is living out her own dreams through her child's success.

In Australia, momanagers are common and celebrity agents think they come with the territory of managing a young star. They are particularly prevalent in the music industry, where young talent is promoted in an adult fashion and lucrative incomes are generated.

'If you're a mum and your kid is a superstar, you can see other people taking over your child's life and encroaching on the traditional maternal role. I think they are getting involved for the right reasons — to make sure their kid is not being ripped off,' says celebrity agent Max Markson.

Silverchair's mothers managed the band until they found a manager they were happy with; Tina Arena's mother managed her at first; Tammin Sursok's dad is involved in her career; and Nikki Webster's mother is pretty hands-on too. Holly Valance's mum, Rachel Stevens, is believed to have been instrumental in sacking her manager Scott Michaelson, who successfully took Holly to court around the time that Delta announced she was leaving Glenn.

"It's a **goal** they had together since Delta was a child, and I have truly never seen **a closer mother and daughter.**"

A friend

Delta with Lea at the 2002 Bastille Day Ball

Delta in concert, Christmas 2002

Internationally, Beyoncé's mother Lili manages her daughter and styles her, while Justin Timberlake's mother Lynne Harless is also heavily involved in his career.

'It doesn't always end in tears, and there are benefits,' says a music insider. 'But they are new managers and often can't see the wood for the trees because they think their kid is the bee's knees.'

An insider agrees that Lea would have found managing Delta a daunting task. 'I do think she is sometimes overwhelmed by the responsibilities of looking after Delta.' But Stephen Harmon, Delta's theatrical agent, says Lea is the best person for the job. 'Her mum absolutely cares so much about her. She's the right person to be the manager. The amount of time and attention to detail is just amazing. Delta doesn't even have to worry about what she's going to wear. I'm glad she's got that job — it's one hell of a job and she helps Delta with decisions on every little step of her career.'

Lecturer Karen Brooks thinks there are pitfalls a mother managing her daughter can easily fall into. 'A mother might naturally think she knows her daughter better than anyone, and as a good mother Lea is protective of her daughter. But her role as manager would always be heavily influenced and possibly overshadowed by her role as Delta's mother. In the case of a parent who is heavily involved in their child's professional life, the lines between professional and personal are continually blurred. They overlap and become very murky. Where does your role as mother and manager begin and end? In other words, the parent becomes a friend, confidant, business manager, partner, employer, employee — the list is endless.

'Part of being a celebrity — or succeeding in any walk of life — is taking risks. How can a mother invite her child to take risks?

How can she continue to support and watch her child putting themselves on the line — if not physically, then certainly emotionally and psychologically. A mother's instinct is to withdraw, shelter and protect . . . and this could well be to the detriment of her child's career. A mother might naturally think she knows her daughter better than anyone . . . and it might even be true. But knowing your daughter and knowing what is best for her, are two different things.'

One mother who knows from experience what Lea faces is the mother of Kate Ceberano, Cherie, who managed Kate for ten years with the assistance of trusted agents and advisors. It is a route that Lea and Delta have now established, with Stephen Harmon handling Australian theatrical offers and an international music agent based in the US (DC Music) to guide her US launch.

Max Markson once remarked that the involvement of specialist agents is a good solution to balancing the demands and opportunities of international stardom with natural protectiveness.

'It's a fine line between a parent looking after a kid and a parent being over-protective and annoying. The intelligent mother would say, "We have to have a manager who knows what to do but I want to be hands-on."'

Will Delta eventually need to assert her independence? And given their present closeness, will Lea find it hard to step back from such an intense relationship as her daughter matures? A music insider warns that stories abound of business partnerships between families and their famous children ending in tears. He cites LeAnn Rimes, who took her father to court to end their business relationship. Brooke Shields and her mother Teri went through a difficult separation, and Britney Spears' mother publicly criticised her daughter for less than virginal behaviour with then boyfriend Justin Timberlake.

Like Britney's mother, Teri Shields was extremely protective of daughter when it came to men. George Michael laughed about the time, before he realised he was gay, he tried to seduce teenage Brooke Shields. He got Brooke home, only to find police tape around her bed and Teri lurking in the corridor.

While Teri is legendary among celebrity mothers, Lea has allowed Delta to explore love. 'She kept a watchful eye on her boyfriends,' says a friend. 'To a certain extent, that's natural protectiveness of any mother. But I think that they are so close, Delta will eventually reach an age when she feels she has to be independent.'

If this happens, Karen Brooks says Lea will grieve. 'Not only will she be "losing" her daughter (which is quite normal in many mother and daughter relationships when the daughter strikes out on her own) but her professional status will also change. If Delta becomes independent of her, Lea will effectively lose her job. Her influence and power will be over. Even her role as mother — which in the traditional sense refers to a younger child — will be all but over. So a great deal of what defines who Lea is, and which relies on Delta's ongoing success and her own part in it, will be denied her. She will be grieving for herself too. Her sense of self will be heavily compromised. It may take her a while to recover. There could be grief and anger, which potentially could impact on their relationship.'

Phyllis Butow says the natural need for independence from parents is especially challenging for those young adults with cancer. 'They have had to become completely dependent again. So they will again go through the separation and independence that probably happened ten years earlier.'

But the mother and daughter team remain incredibly close and Delta can't imagine life without Lea. Clearly tiring of the industry and media's view of her mother as controlling, Delta recently leapt to Lea's defence in an interview with *Daily Telegraph* music columnist and industry authority, Kathy McCabe. Her clear and angry response to what McCabe described as a 'nasty whispering campaign against Lea' was so strong the article was given a pointer on the *Telegraph*'s front page of that edition: 'Delta says "Leave My Mother Alone"'.

A strong girl with a high regard for her own instincts, and harrowed by the trauma of cancer, Delta also no doubt took very personally the implication that she would be so easily manipulated. It was now the cub's turn to protect the lioness.

'She [Lea] does everything with me,' Delta said. 'She handed out lollies to everybody while I was on stage signing autographs during all the in-stores we did. I love her being a part of it,' Delta defended. 'All my parents have ever wanted to do is support me and my ambitions. I have thrown my family into the music industry — they didn't choose. I am still nineteen and there are a lot of things to learn about the music business. Who do I trust? My family, my mum and dad. I'll learn from them and they keep me informed. They also give me the freedom to be creative.

'My poor mum is copping a lot lately and that's not fair because I instigate everything. I say, let's do that and let's not do that. She's just the one who has to deliver the message. She's such a wonderful, strong woman. She was a mother who had to tell the world that her daughter wasn't well.'

As Delta matures, Lea is managing her career while still allowing her daughter to find her own way, trusting her instincts and morals as she did when she was a child. Music industry observers note that Lea is still heavily involved, but is no longer always seen with Delta.

'I like to keep a low profile,' says Lea. 'I don't like to be in the papers.' She initially chaperoned Delta when she first began dating Mark Philippoussis. With the handsome sports star, Delta was blossoming into an independent woman. But it wouldn't be long before her mother had to fly across the world to be with her once more.

“She is such a trooper. The girl will give you her left arm to make it happen. She commits and wants it to be right, and that is her naturally as a person.”

John Brousek
Executive Producer, *Hating Alison Ashley*

CHAPTER 11

Hating Alison Ashley

When Delta returned to Australia, Mark soon followed. Used to girls following him around the circuit, he suddenly had to juggle his schedule with Delta's commitment to return to work.

Delta picked him up in a limousine and they drove straight to her home in Sydney, stopping for petrol on the way and openly embracing at the service station. 'We saw them hugging and holding hands,' says a customer who was there at the time. 'They looked so happy and in love.'

Paparazzi captured their reunion and asked for photos at the airport, then followed them to Delta's home. Mark — just off a plane, dressed in jeans, unshaven and wearing a cap — was particularly unimpressed. Desperate to keep her professional and private life separate, Delta was not keen to showcase her relationship either.

'I know it's part and parcel of our jobs, but sometimes it's overwhelming,' she said of the intense interest in their relationship. Mark was a much bigger star than Blair, and she was now an international success. Privacy was part of the past.

Now separated by their careers and living in different countries, they had made a pact to speak every day. 'Six-dollar-a-minute phone calls — that's the scary part!' Delta joked about the separation caused by the demands of their two careers.

Delta was learning to live again and blossoming beside Mark. But her life was still not balanced. Without work, without song or performance, she wasn't able to feel that life could reach the highs she experienced before cancer. 'She was desperate to work again,' says Delta's theatrical agent, Stephen Harmon.

So when executive producer John Brousek approached Harmon to ask Delta to reconsider the role of Alison in the forthcoming film version of Robin Klein's best-selling young adult book, *Hating Alison Ashley*, Harmon thought that if she was well enough to do it, the film would be the perfect project for her professionally and personally. 'Sony had said no, Wheatley had said no. But I thought it would be good for her to do an Australian film before she got big in the US and went straight to a Hollywood project. I thought it would be good experience for her and also a way to reinforce her love of Australia. And she needed to do something — it was good therapy for her. She's not someone who sits around.'

Stephen Harmon says of his decision to approach Lea and Delta again with the offer, 'The book is an Australian classic and sold over 250,000 copies and is on the school curriculum. Delta really, really wanted to do it, and Lea thought it would be a good idea too. She hadn't worked in months. She was nervous and quite keen to do something because she had time off and was going through all the treatment. She accepted it without even knowing if she was in remission. She knew it would be a challenge, that she'd be very tired and it would be very hard work. And the producers knew that something might happen, she might relapse, so it was a risk to take on the role. But she said that if she had to have more chemo and radiation, she would do that — and do the film as well. Amazing.'

John Brousek was naturally delighted that Delta was finally going to be Alison. The film process, as always in Australia, had been a long and frustrating journey. He had come on board the project three years before, and he and co-producer Elizabeth Howatt-Jackman first noticed Delta on *Neighbours*.

'We were looking around for fresh new talent, we'd seen her

"For a **nineteen-year-old** to play a fourteen- to fifteen-year-old there had to be a **nice person at the heart of the character**. We felt Delta radiated the qualities of the character on screen."

John Brousek
Executive producer, *Hating Alison Ashley*

on *Neighbours* and thought she had a look that suited the film. We had meetings with her and her mother at that time to get a feel for each other, and we all clicked. She is so genuine. But then Delta became more prominent as a singer, and then of course she was sick, so obviously it wasn't possible. And fortunately or unfortunately we lost finance for the film — it was all off.'

But John and Elizabeth didn't give up and when the film was viable again John decided to approach Delta once more. 'I knew it would be a long shot. And of course the film would be made with her or without her . . . let's be realistic. I asked Stephen how Delta was recovering and would she be interested in filming later this year. Delta loved the project and, although she couldn't work full bore, there was a window of opportunity. It's nice when the team you wanted comes together. Erika [played by Saskia Burmeister] and Delta are just perfect.'

The book, an Australian classic by Robin Klein, charts the journey of two girls trying to be the top of the class. Delta has said it is one of her favourite novels and she thought the film was a great way to ease herself back into work.

In the book, the girls Erika and Alison are only eleven, but the film made them older: fourteen or fifteen. 'I think the film has such a great heart and deserved to be done. In the film, the girls are on the cusp, before they know a hardened world. There is innocence,' John says. 'There is a positive moral message in the story, and everybody sees that in the book as well as the film. It is a message about being comfortable with who you are, and finding out who you are.' For John, Delta is the soul of Alison.

Delta signed to the project and, after her holiday in LA, began work wearing a long blonde wig similar to her own hair before the chemotherapy made her locks fall out. John Brousek says that she loved wearing the wig. 'Delta joked that because of the hair, she felt fourteen again.

'Delta's role as Alison was an interesting emotional arc,' he continues. 'She was a girl who obviously had a journey to make, learning about herself and growing into an independent woman. I've directed a lot of theatre and very few people live up to their publicity but after meeting Delta, I found she was as nice as the hype. For a nineteen-year-old to play a fourteen- to fifteen-year-old there had to be a nice person at the heart of the character. We felt Delta radiated the qualities of the character on screen.'

He added that he cast Delta because she was right for the role, not because of her market appeal. 'That would be an abuse of Delta,' John says. After reading the script, Delta asked for the role of Alison to become bigger, to balance with the other role of Erika. 'Every actor asks that,' John says.

'We had many meetings with the executive producer, John Brousek, and talked about the character,' Stephen Harmon explains. 'In the book and original screenplay the character of Alison wasn't as meaty a role as that of the girl who hates Alison [Erica], so Alison was beefed up to make things more balanced.'

The shooting schedule was compacted from seven to five weeks to meet Delta's needs. 'There were a lot of 5 am calls when there wasn't meant to be,' says Stephen. 'John tried his best, but the director was making a film. She didn't complain — of course not, she was so happy to be working again — but it was very tiring for her.'

'She is such a trooper,' says John admiringly. 'The girl will give you her left arm to make it happen. She commits and wants it to be right, and that is her naturally as a person. A feature film is tough. If she needed to stay to finish a scene, Delta was always, "Yes, no problem." She is not a clock watcher. She is a creative person, who understands and is focused on the project.'

The long days on set also meant down time for Delta in her trailer. 'I was on set one day and she was on set at 9 am but not filming until 4. She played music from her new album and we talked and we hung about,' says Stephen. 'For someone as dynamic as her, it was a big adjustment for her after *Neighbours*, which does two-and-a-half hours of drama every week.' But it also helped Delta rest on set.

'She's an incredibly active person. It goes with strong work ethic and motivation,' says John. 'So it was a surprise for her. But when she got the hang of the focus required for acting in a feature film, she found the time useful to work on her character and she knew she had to rest too.'

As usual, Delta spent the time thinking, dreaming, writing — not resting. When she wasn't thinking about Alison, her mind turned, as always, to her music. 'In quieter moments and on weekends she was tinkering . . . and writing music. Delta actually finds it relaxing, and she was so excited and full of great ideas,' says John.

John says that he and Delta developed a strong friendship through making the film. 'On film sets, you become so close so quickly and you have an honest relationship. There are a lot of things to work through and you get to know each other quickly. She really is a sweetheart, but there's a vulnerable side to her personality that the public doesn't see.

'I think everyone feels protective of her. Delta is a knockout in the film and totally credible. People are always looking to knock the tall poppy, and a lot of singers have tried to do films and not done it well. But I think people will be very, very surprised. Saskia is brilliant in her role, and Delta was surrounded by people who helped her as it was a fantastic cast.'

John was also conscious of Delta's fame as a singer and made sure that the film showcased her acting talent, and that alone. 'I think this film is a vehicle for Delta as an actor and adds another string to her bow. This is an acting job, not a singing job. This is a good Australian film that is well made and has a lot of talented people working on it.'

While Delta was the biggest star on set in terms of popularity, the crew soon discovered that Delta was not a diva who demanded super-luxurious sheets and celebrity chefs in her trailer.

'She was such a pleasure on set. We had hundreds of extras. One day, after she had been resting in her trailer, she just came out and met everyone and sang them a song . . . totally impromptu. That is how giving she is, how generous of spirit . . . it was a special moment and sums up how she was on set,' says John Brousek.

Australian comedian and actress, Jean Kittson, plays opposite Delta in the film and also went to LA to interview her for *OK!* magazine's first Australian issue. Jean remembers she brought her teenage daughter, Victoria, on set during filming and Delta promptly invited Victoria into her trailer.

'That's the equivalent of someone of my generation having John Lennon hang out of his trailer and say, "Hey, I'm having trouble with this *Imagine* thing . . . D'ya wanna help?"' Jean described Delta as 'translucent and elfin'. 'I was astonished by her ability to juggle at least two careers while maintaining her genuine warmth and generosity.'

"Why wouldn't he want to be with Delta? Delta is beautiful, wonderful, and talented. Being a romantic, I totally understand why Mark wants to spend all his time with her. I'm jealous."

John Alexander

The crew were just as impressed with Delta. 'Crews are tough judges. They are hardened. They took her to their hearts,' remarks John. 'She was totally unpretentious and there was no rhubarb, Delta was everybody's friend. She knew she was the least experienced there and she took that on board. She was eager to learn and understand. She was giving, inquisitive and wanted to know about how everything worked. She and Saskia would be sitting with everyone at lunchtime.'

Delta got a chance to reunite with her school friend, Rachael Carpani. When the two later met up with their school's media director, Elisabeth Pellinkhof, they told her they both adored playing the roles of rebellious adolescents.

With Craig McLachlan, another *Neighbours* graduate, Delta bonded instantly. 'They are poles apart musically and there was plenty of fun to be had,' says John of Delta and Craig. 'A lot of singing. Delta bursts into song all the time. All the actors were great. Some movies are like war zones, but this was a sweet film.'

For Delta, some of her down time was spent with Mark after he returned to Australia. An aspiring actor himself, he was not doing a cameo in the film, according to the director, but loved to come on set to be with her. 'Her face lit up when he came in,' says John fondly. 'It was nice to see them happy together.'

As Delta was committed to long days of filming, she and Mark found it hard to be together. They turned up at Bells Beach for a surf tournament. When the event was cancelled because of lack of waves, they strolled along the beach hand in hand and openly cuddled, to the delight of the other spectators. Delta taught Mark her songs and Mark energetically 'slaughtered' them.

Lea increasingly allowed the couple to be by themselves,

trusting that Mark was truly in love with her daughter. 'They both know what they've got is really special,' a friend declared. 'This isn't some fling and they're not going to let anything get in their way.'

But the intense scrutiny was sometimes hard for the couple, and they were now half-seriously being called 'Australia's Posh and Becks'. With Mark joking he now worried about what to wear when they went out together on dates, she made the effort to face the cameras and support him at matches.

Mark wanted to be by her side as she made her first public appearance since the ARIAs, at the 2004 Logies in May. Only nineteen, Delta had been nominated for a Gold Logie, the top television award in the country. Mark is thought to have declined to play at the prestigious clay court tournament in Monte Carlo to be with Delta on her big night in the spotlight. It was also their first official outing together.

When they arrived on the red carpet, it was the arrival of Australia's super couple.

Designer Peter Morrissey dressed her for the event, doing the fittings at her trailer on the set of *Hating Alison Ashley*. 'She was like a swan. She wanted to look beautiful for her man,' he said of the excitement leading up to the big night and his creation of the stunning black dress.

Her mum worked closely with Morrissey so Delta could concentrate on the film. Says Stephen Harmon, 'Her mum arranges all her clothes. Delta doesn't have to think about it — she's an artist. She wouldn't have worried about what she was going to wear to the Logies at all.'

The jersey gown was designed in conjunction with celebrity jeweller Cerrone, who added three-million-dollars worth of diamonds to the dress along with matching earrings and bracelet. In a suitably Posh-and-Becks-esque appearance (but far more stylish), Mark matched Delta in a black suit and diamond accessories.

'She looks stunning and gorgeous,' Mark said proudly as he escorted her on the red carpet. 'I'm very proud of her.' A glowing, waif-like Delta said simply, 'He's terrific, isn't he? I think I should take him home.'

There was also a massive diamond ring that Delta wore on her right hand. It immediately sparked speculation that Mark had proposed. Delta giggled on the red carpet that the ring was in fact lent from Cerrone.

Still, the ring was enough to inspire discussion about how serious the relationship between Delta and Mark had become after just a few months. It was suggested that the fact it was worn on her right hand instead of her left was simply a red herring, given that Danielle Spencer — a mutual friend through producer Vince Pizzinga — had worn her ring on her right hand for some time, to keep her engagement to Russell Crowe under wraps before they were ready to make an announcement.

A family friend assured *New Idea* they weren't engaged because Delta wouldn't have been able to keep it a secret. Another friend added that Lea wouldn't be keen on her daughter being engaged so young. The timing also made it unlikely. 'She's just beginning to make her comeback and desperately wants to make it in America,' a source told *New Idea*. 'But they're great together, they're having a good time and they're barely apart.'

At the Logies, Delta and Mark took their place at the *Neighbours* table. Ex-boyfriend Blair was seated elsewhere so as not to place the couple in any awkward photos. But while Delta was the undisputed star of the night, both her Logie nominations went elsewhere.

McLeod's Daughters star Lisa Chappell won Best Actress. She was so surprised to beat Delta, she'd said she was going to drink all night because there was such a remote chance she would have to get up on stage.

The Gold Logie went to Ten's variety star, Rove McManus, who dedicated it to his girlfriend Belinda Emmett — a friend of Delta's who is also battling cancer. Rove was stunned to beat the favourite, Delta, joking on the red carpet he didn't have a 'gibbon's arse chance in hell of beating her'.

'Delta didn't want to win the Gold Logie, she wanted Rove to win,' says Stephen Harmon. 'She was so honoured to be nominated, but she didn't think it was appropriate that she won a Gold Logie when she'd hardly been on television that year.'

Peter Wynne, executive producer of the Logies, said he found out she hadn't won hours before the telecast and was surprised at the results, but Delta was happy Rove had won the Gold Logie and pleased just to be well enough to attend the night.

She also appeared to be very relaxed and at ease with the attention. She explained that she wasn't as nervous as she had been the previous year. 'I was petrified. Now, I'm happy to be here,' she said on the night.

She also laughed about how her shoe strap kept coming undone, forcing an assistant to continually help her readjust it. 'I think it's a tradition now with the Logies. I figure the dress ripped last year so I may as well have shoe problems — it's unbelievable!'

Seeing her that night, Mark Holden was thrilled at how beautiful she looked. 'The Scudrems' arrival on the red carpet was huge,' he wrote excitedly on his website diary. 'Delta looked radiant with her new natural brown short hair and a fair-dinkum boyfriend. It's brilliant to see her out and about again with a big, strapping bloke on her arm. Fantastic! No gold, but plenty of golden moments, especially her dance with Rove . . . beautiful.'

Psychic Georgina Walker was also struck by seeing them together. 'Brushing past me at the recent Logies, I could feel Delta Goodrem's new-found strength. But she reminds me so much of a porcelain doll that needs to be held, cared for and treasured. The sparks of energy were jumping back and forth between her and boyfriend Mark Philippoussis. She is the water for his soul. At last he has found someone that understands the fame game.

'Mark feels strength in this match. He has found a woman who gives and receives support and affection. Their commitment will endure if they allow each other freedom to have periods of time apart while following their careers.'

Mark left the day after the Logies to fly back to the US, pointedly telling reporters he would not be up late partying because he 'doesn't do messy anymore'. While the Logie accolade would have nicely complemented her seven ARIAs, Delta was more concerned about winning the battle against Hodgkin's disease, finishing her album, showcasing to Sony executives in the US, and supporting Mark as he suffered an increasingly bewildering loss of form.

In a candid interview on the eve of the French Open in Roland Garros, Paris, Mark Philippoussis admitted that the off-court dramas had made him lose focus. 'My mind wasn't on the court — my heart wasn't there. What happened hit me hard. I'm a pretty relaxed guy, maybe I should be a bit more of — is it nice to say?— an arsehole. But that's just the type of guy I am,' Mark said.

The couple still had to contend with the view that Delta might be distracting Mark from his tennis, but they were also heartened by some of tennis's most respected figures voicing their support for him and his relationship. 'You'd be more worried if a bloke didn't have a girlfriend,' said Wally Masur, a long-time friend of Mark's.

John Alexander also went on the record in support of Mark. 'People tend to forget that Mark came back from three knee surgeries, which could have ended the career of many other athletes, to become a Wimbledon finalist and win a second Davis Cup for his country. There's no doubt a stable relationship is a great basis for life. If Delta supports Mark, it can't do anything but help.

'Why wouldn't he want to be with Delta? Delta is beautiful, wonderful, and talented. Being a romantic, I totally understand why Mark wants to spend all his time with her. I'm jealous. He will bounce back on court, as he is so talented. He is entitled to a personal life and he needs to balance that with his professional life.'

Delta tried to rise above the criticism, but said it still upset her. 'I can't lie and say it doesn't hurt,' she said. But she continued to openly show her support by attending his matches, and Mark was grateful for her presence as he continued to lose.

'Tennis is not an easy sport,' he said. 'Negativity does crawl in there.' Then, echoing his girlfriend's mantra, Mark added, 'As long as you stay positive, things turn around. Everybody — my girlfriend, my father, definitely my father, my fitness trainer — they've all been very positive. Everybody was so positive, saying, "It's gonna come, you just have to work hard, it's going to pay off."'

'It's a tough world, but it's made me the person I am too,' Mark reflects. 'You learn from everything. You learn from your mistakes. You learn from the negative things. I'm still learning. I'm still a young guy. I'm learning every day and that makes me stronger.'

After a few months by Mark's side, Delta came to understand his moods and personality. She realised that, like her, he passionately experienced highs and lows in his career and personal life. But unlike Delta, Mark tended to brood.

They claimed they were both performers — he on the court and she on the stage — and that they both felt nervous when they stepped into their respective arenas. 'I'm very proud to be with her. She's inspiring,' Mark said. 'I've been through a lot for my age too, and she's an incredibly strong person.'

'We've both been talking about it and visualising and thinking positive thoughts,' Delta said in Paris. 'Just staying positive is the real key thing. He doesn't shout back. He doesn't retaliate. He just takes it, and says he wants to focus on tennis. We've talked together, you know, and we know you have your highs and your lows and you've got to accept the good days and the bad days.'

Increasingly devoting herself to work again, Delta still stuck by her vow to live life more fully as well. She made time to meet Mark in the romantic city of Paris, where he competed in the French Open. But still nervous about her voice, she reportedly pulled out of a singing appearance at the Australian Embassy because Mark was unable to be with her.

Whereas her mother had always in the past been the one she wanted by her side (and she continued to need her), Delta still felt vulnerable and fragile, and didn't want to sing without Mark's presence. She remained worried about the quality of her voice, mindful of the specialist's warning ringing in her head that it could sound 'different'. A friend said that she pulled out because it was 'all too much'.

Delta was still learning to take it easy, to restrain her natural urge to push herself as she could before. She was also about to have her eyes opened to the uglier side of fame.

"Delta has learned: where there's a hit, there's a writ."

Rachael Brown
Sun Herald

Paul Higgins with the first recordings of Delta, shown on screen

Delta performing with Brian McFadden

CHAPTER 12

The Love Rat

Delta was now an international star, a cancer survivor and one half of a celebrity couple that excited such interest there were photographers nearly everywhere they went. She accepted it as part of her life if she wanted to perform on the world stage.

But Delta, everybody's friend and sweetheart, never expected one of her own to turn against her, or to find herself embroiled in a very public and embarrassing court case with people she once trusted with her career.

In Australia, Delta always had a brilliant relationship with the media, because of her personality, her age, the way she fought her illness and – not least – her professional achievements. Her brave and beautiful appearance in pink on the red carpet at the 2003 ARIAs and her elfin turn in black at the 2004 Logies with Mark on her arm underlined how revered she was now by the Australian public.

'Unlike other celebrities who must be resigned to the fact that good coverage comes with the bad, few people (except for Guy Sebastian) can rival Delta's squeaky-clean image,' quipped a columnist on the eve of the Logies. 'Find a bad word written about her and I'll find you an ugly farmer on *McLeod's Daughters*. Throughout the entire ordeal, Delta has not begged for pity, she has been a picture of bravery, poise and devotion to her friends and family.'

Her friends were loyal. Her clean-living lifestyle, moral judgement and sound decisions with her mother meant there was nothing that could drag her image into the gutter. She simply worked too hard, cared too much and thought too much about her decisions and her position as a role model. Even with her breakups she maintained a dignified front.

Jay Till, however, was still in love with the star. 'He was her boyfriend when she was fifteen, that's it,' Lea says of the man now known as 'The Love Rat'.

When Jay was first thinking of selling his story, a friend of his acted as the intermediary and emailed the Sydney newspapers (who rarely pay) and *News of the World* (who pay and pay well when they want a feature). Frank Thorne, leading Fleet Street journalist and Sydney stringer for the UK tabloids, was told by the *News of the World* to follow up the story. 'He poured out his heart to me,' says Frank.

Jay told Frank that he and Delta had been boyfriend and girlfriend when Delta was fifteen, and had reunited during her cancer treatment. He had given her a Louis Vuitton bag for Christmas and claimed he had the receipt for the bag as proof. He told Frank that, to their friends, they were the 'golden couple' and he had helped her through her worst days of treatment.

'When she was diagnosed with cancer, I was there for her,' Jay claimed to Frank. 'I was Delta's support throughout and, as far as I was concerned, we were an item.'

Whether or not Jay read more into his friendship with Delta than ever existed, he alleged he'd been dumped by Delta for Mark Philippoussis. As part of the deal, he offered Frank love letters, photos, tender cards and lyrics he said were dedicated to him. But he was most upset and angry about the expensive bag. 'The next time I saw the bag was in a photograph of Mark and Delta,' Jay told Frank. 'Delta's handbag was in one hand, and Philippoussis on the other.'

While Jay negotiated, Delta was in the US showcasing for Sony executives. Then she flew to meet Mark in London for Wimbledon, to support him during his most important tournament.

Says Frank, '*News of the World* was interested because it was

"People are always looking to knock the tall poppy."

John Brousek

topical, with the tennis coming up and her boyfriend being Scud. So they called me and told me to give him a call. I said I'd give *Woman's Day* a call and do the story for them and also *News of the World*. It was a favour to him really, because *News of the World* only wanted to pay peanuts.

'I held off on doing the story for *News of the World* while *Woman's Day* got their act together. They wanted to pay him $45,000. I spoke to him an hour before he went to the *Woman's Day* office, then suddenly afterwards he wasn't available and I realised what had happened – they'd kidnapped him and tried to cut me out of the story! So this is my bloody story – I'm furious!'

Hell hath no fury like a Fleet Street journalist scorned. Frank Thorne continues, 'I send a photographer to doorstop him and take his picture, and then decide to throw a grenade in. I ring Sony Music and ask them, "So what do you reckon about this ex-boyfriend of Delta's trying to sell her love letters for $40,000?"'

It was the first time Delta had experienced a kiss-and-tell and the family's reaction was fast and furious. Sony immediately informed Lea. Never one to do things by halves, Lea called James Packer, chairman of Australian Consolidated Press which owns *Woman's Day*, and explained that Delta was in far too delicate a condition to cope with such betrayal and lurid details of her personal life sprayed across the papers. Sympathetic, James asked *Woman's Day* to drop the feature.

'I never would have made a call to Sony like that if I was doing the story, because I knew what would happen from experience,' Frank says. In the meantime he sold the story with a new Love Rat angle to rival publication *New Idea*. The magazine ran the cover: 'Delta betrayed'.

It couldn't have turned out better for Delta. Jay was crucified by the Australian newspapers. Frank managed to sell the story to the *Daily Mirror* because Mark Philippoussis was still in Wimbledon. It was going to be a big spread in the papers that weekend but Marlon Brando died, Mark was finished in the tennis, and so the story was dumped.

God was watching over Delta, just as her mother had always said. Jay did a brief appearance on *Today Tonight*, which ran the Love Rat angle too. Lea was reportedly pleased by the outcome of the story. Delta maintained her dignity, as always, but both she and Lea were shaken by the experience and shocked by this betrayal by one of their inner circle.

Mark understood, having endured the embarrassment of former teenage lover, Melanie Maudran, doing a hurtful kiss-and-tell to British newspapers, disclosing intimate details of their romance after they'd split up. 'I've been very hurt growing up,' Mark reflected once. Now he says he is very protective of those he loves.

It has become more and more apparent that people are either devoted to Delta or trying to sue her.

The biggest headache for the newly formed Goodrem Management was the court case against Higgins and Carter, who were then fighting to release her first album and video, and were alleging that Delta and her parents had breached an agreement made in June and July 1999. They were demanding ten per cent of Delta's earnings on her first two albums. The music industry watched in disbelief as agents for the pair tried to find Goodrem so they could serve a writ on her as she flitted around the world. 'It's all turned ugly, but that is life,' said Lea Goodrem. Delta said on her website that she was 'sad' about the turn of events.

Higgins and Carter broadcast to the press their involvement with Delta, claiming, 'She is the biggest act in Australia because of all the groundwork we put in. But we were never given credit for that.' They then went quiet as they commenced formal legal action and served Delta and her mother with a court summons.

This court case was a reminder to Delta that because of her stunning success and strong personality, she is no longer regarded as an innocent young teen singer and actress, but a woman and a superstar. When her lawyer asked the magistrate to dismiss the case, saying Delta was 'of far too tender years for litigation', the magistrate answered, 'She has survived in the harsh world of entertainment.'

Some people estimated that Higgins and Carter would be awarded fifteen million dollars; this dispute was ultimately settled out of court. Her first album will not be released.

'Delta is not a child,' says Karen Brooks. 'I know it defines a role, but it also places her in a very subordinate position, and almost gives her permission to be excessively protected, managed and whatever else a child needs. However, she is a beautiful and successful young woman; an actor, a singer and a survivor of cancer.'

The Goodrems were not only asking for the CD not to be released, but that a three-minute video from that time (in which she serenaded a teddy bear) also be destroyed, in a legal move dubbed a 'Bad Hair Defence' by the press. Ever dignified, Delta concentrated on finishing her single, video and album release.

The split with Wheatley was ugly, divisive and bitter. Delta was painfully reminded of her decision to cut her ties with Wheatley when there was a hot public debate about whether she'd thanked him properly after the ARIAs. She quickly reassured her fans on her website that she was very grateful for all Wheatley had done. But Wheatley was stung, and his supporters and music critics made sure his dissent was known.

'It was the first time Delta felt the ill wind of criticism,' says crikey.com's music observer Max Factor. While Delta made every effort to dampen the drama – including writing on her website that she had not ditched anyone, as a response to fans' concerns – this controversy still bubbles below the surface, and Farnham recently made pointed comments about loyalty which were interpreted to be aimed at Delta for changing her management.

Mark Holden is embarrassed that he too is now embroiled in the anti-Delta camp because of his action against Sony for non-payment of consultancy fees. He urgently released a press statement after the story broke that he too was suing Delta. 'He tried to be discreet for Delta's sake,' says a source close to Holden. 'But it has all come out now.'

In the public statement, Holden challenged the reports that he was taking legal action against Delta. 'This is completely wrong,' Holden said. 'In 2000, Sony Australia asked me to assist them looking for new artists by listening to the many demos that existed in their A and R (Artist and Repertoire) department. Among the many CDs from hopeful artists, I heard one submitted by Delta Goodrem. I presented it to the management at Sony. Subsequently, my company concluded an A and R consultancy agreement with Sony to provide them with services related to the Delta project. Issues have developed regarding payment for these services which we have been seeking to negotiate with Sony for some time. We are currently in the process of resolving the matter. We do not have any legal issues with Delta or her mother Lea. We wish them health, happiness and success.'

To top it all off, Delta has also had to contend with being blamed for the marriage break-up of British pop star Brian McFadden, with whom she had recorded a duet. McFadden's wife Kerry was the winner on the reality TV show, *I'm A Celebrity – Get Me Out Of Here!* which was watched by over 12 million people. The UK papers claimed her husband dumped her via a phone call because he was obsessed with Delta Goodrem and was 'pouring out his heart to her in up to ten phone calls a day'.

Delta was dragged into the mess of McFadden's high-profile split with UK sweetheart Kerry Katona (she no longer uses McFadden) after he revealed that his relationship with Delta started at a Royal Variety Concert in London in December 2004. 'She couldn't stop giggling at him,' said a backstage observer.

In an exclusive with *News of the World*, Brian categorically denied he was involved with Delta. He and Kerry then spoke candidly of their painful break-up. The *Sun* newspaper claimed, 'Brian adores Delta. He thinks she is the best thing that ever happened to him and he can't stop talking about her. Brian's completely infatuated and rings her all the time.'

Said Lea, exasperated, 'Honestly!'

McFadden's bad boy boozy ways has many fearing he's not what the doctor ordered for Delta. McFadden once admitted 'I was drunk for three months' and he is continuing to turn to the bottle because of his guilt over the marriage breakdown, which has left his ex-wife in the celebrity rehab clinic The Priory.

Delta's friends have expressed concern that she is vulnerable and that she goes for men who always 'let her down'. There are also fears that, stung by party girl Paris Hilton's claims that she was boring, Delta may indulge for the first time in some bad behaviour of her own. Brian said Delta was a little bit drunk when they first became romantic. 'We feel she's trying to keep up with him,' said a friend. 'She doesn't want to be seen as dull.'

The scandal might also be damaging Delta's image in the important UK market when she is trying to establish herself as a global star. A music industry source says, 'Her record company is concerned about how the accusations of marriage wrecking may harm sales but the accusations are untrue. I'll be surprised if it lasts because of the pressure she's already feeling.'

'My immediate thought is it is a high risk relationship,' says psychologist Melanie Price. 'The potential for things going wrong is high — I mean if you are dating someone with that background, the chances of a serene journey are quite low. And in the short term, she has to be very careful for herself — it is more stress for her in an already stressful life But she is a young girl. If she feels well enough to do work and love — and there is no reason not to — she should go for it. She seems to know she needs to look after herself and she has a good support base with her mum looking after her. The old saying is "everything in moderation". I would say to Delta — live it up but remember what you have gone through.'

'There are niggles all over the place now,' says a disappointed source. 'You'd be surprised how negative people are,' sighs Delta's mother. One columnist, Rex Jory, even said that he was 'bored' with Delta.

But through everything, Delta's fans remain loyal and adoring. In a reminder of how much they mean to her, Delta surprised her one millionth fan, seven-year-old Vanessa Aguis, at Sony studios when the fan was taken there on a 'tour'. Discovering Vanessa loved to play the piano, they played together and Delta sang *Lost Without You* in Spanish. 'She is very nice and very pretty,' an ecstatic Vanessa declared. Delta also continues to quietly visit her Starlight Children's Foundation children, and struggles to meet all the requests from sick kids across Australia.

Is the tall poppy syndrome at work in Australia because of Delta's incredible success? Or is not even Delta immune from betrayals, bitterness, cash-grabbing and legal fallouts? Was it always going to happen but perhaps, because of her illness, she enjoyed a honeymoon with fame for longer than is normally granted to other stars?

'People are always looking to knock the tall poppy,' says John Brousek, proud of Delta's achievements and performance in *Hating Alison Ashley*. Rachael Browne of the *Sun Herald* summed up the answer when she quipped, 'Delta has learned: where there's a hit, there's a writ.'

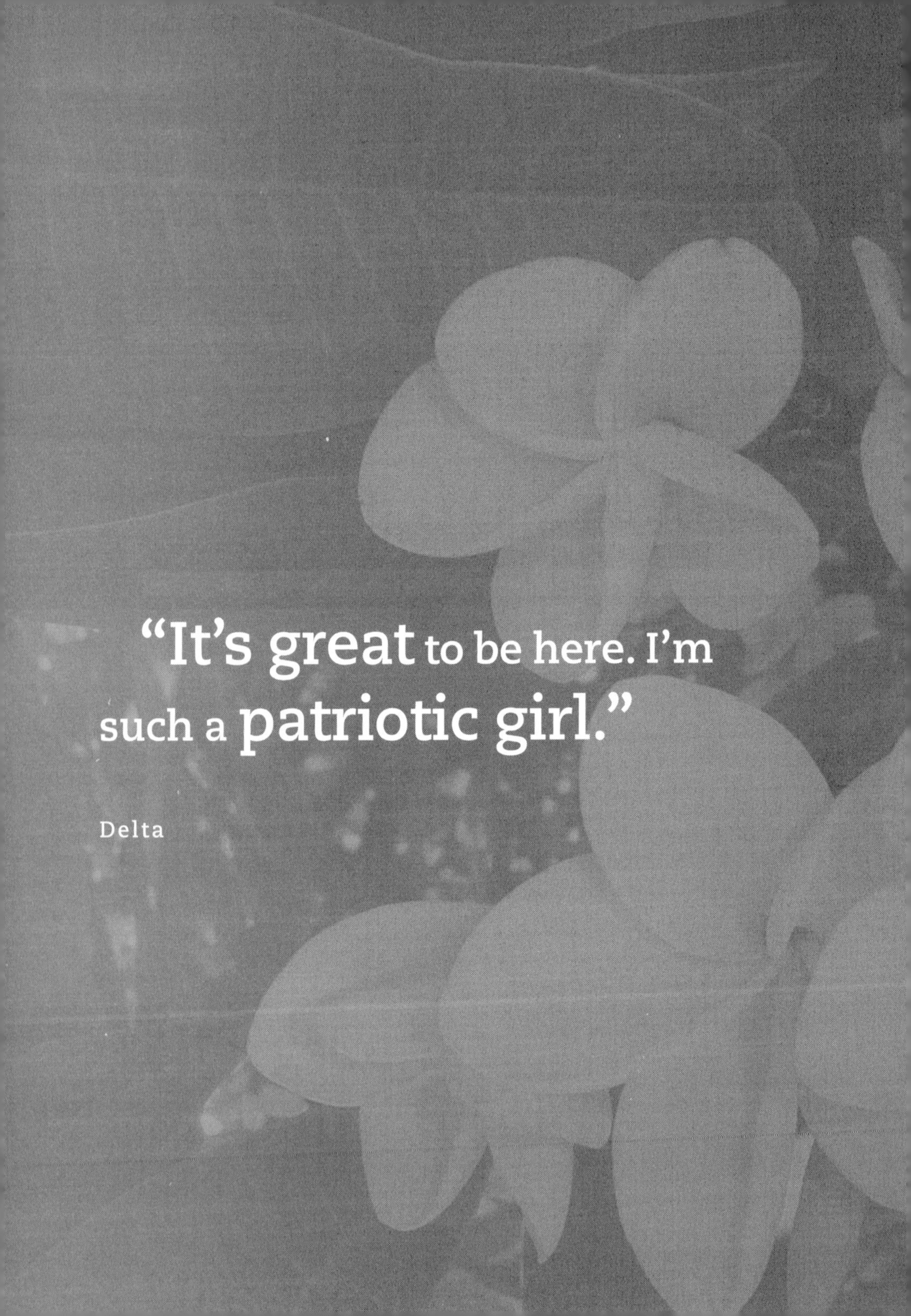

"It's great to be here. I'm such a patriotic girl."

Delta

CHAPTER 13

Back in the Limelight

It was like old times. Delta was back on the set of *Neighbours*, tearfully hugging the crew and co-stars.

'I think everyone was pleased to see her back,' says Ben Michaels. 'She'd started as a kid with potential, and had come back the biggest recording star this country had ever produced. And she'd beaten cancer — an amazing journey.'

Stephen Harmon organised her return to *Neighbours*. 'She wanted to go back. It was very important to her to finish the character [Nina Tucker] properly and give the show back what she felt she owed them. *Neighbours* was great for her profile,' he says.

'They asked for a week, but Lea said to me she could only give them three days. It was hard for them, and they didn't get much notice, but they made it happen and managed to stretch those three days of filming over episodes shown over a few weeks. They would have her back for as long as Delta wanted to be on the show.'

As someone who always feels things deeply, Delta described her return to *Neighbours* as very emotional and uplifting. She had left so suddenly that returning provided her with closure on an important chapter in her life. 'It was so special to go back on set. I couldn't wait to go back. I was so excited. I really felt that Nina and myself had a lot of unfinished business there. It was great to be back around my friends and castmates. It was beautiful.'

Ever the professional, she asked for scripts that would lead up to her return to filming, to ensure she was up to speed with the soap's story-lines as well as her own. She was also pleased that, like her, Nina had been on a journey.

When Nina had left, she had been rattled by her mother's new relationship and torn between Connor (Patrick Harvey), who loved her, and her still intense attraction to Jack (Jay Bunyan). She had fled to her father in India.

The scriptwriting team had sent her to Bollywood to be with her father, and to become an actress. In an echo of Delta's own life, Nina returned from India a huge star. She even had a personal assistant called Krishna.

In a wonderful re-entry to the show, Nina arrives with a new haircut, a fabulous convertible and Krishna. She is also confident and passionate, and for the first time initiates a kiss with Jack, who she believes is her soul mate.

'She came back a lot stronger and confident. Not so timid and vulnerable. She's taken control of her life. I think she had to grow up. If she didn't come back older and wiser then she wouldn't have learnt and grown from what's gone on in the year that she's been missing,' Delta said of Nina's development.

On set, she joked to *TV Week* that she 'mucked up her lines' a few times, as she normally did, and she felt 'rusty'.

The three-day shoot was also intense, but Delta welcomed the workload. 'I liked it,' she told *TV Week*. 'It was more of a roll. I was a little Nina-ed out, but at the same time I'd missed her so much it was great to see her.'

Delta described the last day on her whirlwind shoot as just as teary as her welcome. 'I said to the producers, please make it so I can come back to the show! I love it! Hopefully, if I can give *Neighbours* enough notice, we can get Nina back there again. I really liked the story-line that she came out on — it's really romantic. Ramsay Street will always feel like my Melbourne home. I look at it in such a positive light. To be part of it again was just great.'

Delta's schedule began filling up as she gained strength. She was heartened that the offers were pouring in again now she was well enough to work, and she also wanted to complete deals that had started before her diagnosis. She described her new-found energy as 'precious'.

Around the time of the Logies, the new-look Delta burst onto billboards and she appeared in a TV commercial for soft-drink giant Pepsi, just as Mark Philippoussis had done before her. It was a shrewd and lucrative way to boost her profile again, with Delta commanding a rumoured fee of $300,000 to do the campaign.

'Before Delta got sick, we were looking to launch her for the Dare For More campaign,' says Pepsi's Tony Thomas. 'Then she got sick and needed to recuperate. We wanted her to rest as much as she could until she was better, and then, when she got through her probation period, we were able to shoot.'

Delta was so thrilled with the Pepsi posters she took photos of them for her album. 'This wasn't planned,' she said of her involvement with Pepsi. Much was made about the fact that Mark had also been signed by the soft-drink giant as a celebrity face and was appearing on posters in the lead-up to Delta's adverts. But Delta said it was a coincidence. Ever the cheerleader, she also said she could relate to the Dare For More campaign. 'Dare For More. For me, it relates to daring to be yourself, setting goals and working to achieve them.'

She was thrilled to be working again, but her mother pleaded with her not to overdo it and to rest. While very proud of Delta's work ethic, Lea says that the main problem was getting Delta to stop working when she needed a break.

Within months, Delta was travelling around the world again, either to work on her album or meet up with Mark. When apart,

"Ramsay Street will always feel like my Melbourne home. I look at it in such a positive light. To be part of it again was just great."

Delta

the two spoke every day and Delta put a picture of them together on her mobile phone. Mark carried the photo of him and Delta with his dogs in his wallet.

While Delta adored returning to *Neighbours* and her time on *Hating Alison Ashley*, her first passion was still her music, just as it had always been since she was a little girl. 'I enjoyed the film, but now I want to focus on my music,' Delta said.

It was so important to her, Stephen Harmon says, that she always considered the impact on her music schedule before accepting any other work or endorsements. 'Delta was asked to audition for *Eucalyptus*, the Australian film that even at that early stage already boasted a star of the power of Russell Crowe. It was an offer to audition, not an offer for the part. We looked at the filming dates to see if it could happen, but Delta couldn't do it because she wanted to promote her album.' Nicole Kidman has now accepted the role, and it has been revised for an older woman.

Of all her work commitments, to sing again gave Delta the most joy. She had a low-key return to singing at a function in Brisbane. Thrilled to be on stage, Delta kicked off her silver stilettos after the first song and performed a dozen more to the guests.

Her song writing also had the intensity that Vince Pizzinga anticipated. Of her album, Delta wrote, 'I knew it had to be deeper and darker. I wanted my album to be big, dramatic and truthful, because that's how my year has been.'

'It is going to be a different album, because she's now older. The first album was when she was sixteen or seventeen,' Vince reflected before the album's release. 'She's grown up a lot. I'm sure the sorts of things she wants to talk about will be more profound, given her experiences in the last six to twelve months.'

With her trademark honesty, Delta wrote for her new album about her diagnosis with a song titled *Extraordinary Day*, about the day — 8 July 2003 — when her mother walked into her studio and told her she had Hodgkin's disease. She says that even through the shock of cancer diagnosis, she realised it would be a rich vein for her song writing. Delta was struck by finding out the diagnosis in what she has always called her sanctuary — her studio — and not where one would expect to, such as in a clinic or doctor's rooms. 'I wouldn't be honest if I didn't talk about it in the songs,' Delta says.

And while in LA, Delta wrote a song for Mark called *Out of the Blue* with Guy Chambers, best known for his work with Robbie Williams. The song had such meaning for her and was so uplifting, she chose it for her first new release of material since the diagnosis.

Just as *Not Me, Not I* revealed her heartbreak, Delta's love for Mark and the happiness they had shared since meeting was now revealed through her song writing.

'I did have a relationship in mind when I wrote it,' Delta said. 'When someone comes into your life and takes you from a dark place to a much brighter world, it was a really positive experience. For someone to come into my world and then be able to write about it . . . that was great. When you meet that special someone, it's a wonderful thing. I wanted a song with a sentiment like that.'

The song, and Delta's love and support, undoubtedly raised Mark's spirits as he (and his tennis fans) became increasingly frustrated by his lack of form. At Wimbledon, his favourite tournament, Mark rallied with Delta publicly in the stands watching his every game. But the title eluded him.

He and Delta instead focused on something they were both thrilled to be part of: the Olympics in Athens. A life-long sports nut,

Delta was excited to be invited to perform at a private party for the Australian Olympic team, with her boyfriend playing in the Olympic tennis matches. It was a hedonistic location in an ancient city, at the most important sporting event in the world. For Mark the location was incredibly promising: as a Greek-Australian, what better time than this to regain his place in the sun as one of the gods of tennis?

Delta worked intensely on her album in Sydney until the Olympics while Mark was in the US. Just before she left for Athens, she and her family watched her brother Trent play AFL football at Macquarie University for the East Coast Eagles, and Delta enchanted her brother's team-mates when she joined them for their victory celebrations. For that afternoon, she was Delta the supportive sister, and she is sure that Trent will one day emerge from the shadow of her success.

The next day, Delta was a star again. She was photographed leaving for the Games in a pink overcoat and sunglasses, carrying her Louis Vuitton luggage. 'She looks like a superstar now,' said a friend of her sleek and glamorous appearances in public. Her short curls also gave her a more sophisticated look.

But her smile couldn't contain her excitement at going to the Olympics and reuniting with Mark. 'It's such a huge honour to be here,' she said on arrival in Greece. 'I'm feeling a little jet-lagged right now. It's been a long flight to Athens, but it's great to be here. I'm such a patriotic girl.'

Athens was a city celebrating its Olympic moment. It was a joyous and beautiful place to have a reunion. 'The atmosphere was buzzing,' says Antonia Moskos, an Australian with Greek heritage who attended the Games as well as the reception for the Australian athletes. 'The *plaka* was crammed with people — there was free live music in the squares and everyone was very proud.'

Because of the timing, Delta and Mark couldn't see each other until her performance at the party for the Australian Olympic team. The exhaustion and nerves built inside her as she stepped onto the stage. That hot August night under an Athens sky became one of the most memorable performances of Delta's career.

The Olympic team met her with a roar of approval. They were Australia's best athletes, but that night they were besotted fans of Australia's golden singer. They admired her strength, courage, tenacity and beauty. She was their Greek goddess, but as she sang *Born To Try*, *Lost Without You* and the national anthem, their goddess looked at Mark and began to cry. It was the first time he'd ever seen her perform live.

'The atmosphere at the reception was electric and superb. She came across as so beautiful. She looked radiant in a flowing white halter dress,' Antonia said. 'Stunning, very feminine and so elegant. I think we were all emotional watching her. She looked very proud to have the privilege to sing, and she performed so perfectly. She looked so happy.'

That night, Antonia met Mark and Delta fleetingly. 'They looked gorgeous together. She had a wonderful, beautiful aura, and he was warm and friendly and willing to be photographed.' The happiness Mark felt was apparent after the performance when Delta and Mark nestled in a quiet corner of the reception. Their affection was unbridled and so beautiful for all those there on the night to see. The young couple had the world at their feet, but when they reunited they were lost in their own world of romance.

Mark leaned his head of curls on Delta's shoulder and a photographer captured her putting a tender hand on his neck. 'He was beaming through the entire performance — he couldn't take his eyes off her,' says one onlooker at the function. Mark said simply, 'It was great.'

But for Delta the performance and emotion of seeing Mark took a dramatic turn later that night, when she woke exhausted and suffering from a fever. Ever mindful of her daughter's delicate state, Lea took her to hospital for checks. It was an upsetting end to a beautiful night, and Delta was distressed to hear the next day's front pages were about her 'hospital shock' instead of about the athletes.

Mark was with Delta at the hospital and went straight to see her after a practice session. 'She's fine, she's had a long and big week back in Australia,' he said. 'Coming here and performing was a lot for her. A lot of excitement and nerves at the same time. She was up this morning exhausted with a fever. Fortunately, they brought her in to the hospital to make sure everything is fine. She just needs to have some rest . . . that's all.'

'She was so excited and honoured to sing for the athletes . . . and then to have that happen, she was so embarrassed,' said Lea.

'I just wanted to have a little rest,' Delta said, frustrated at the turn of events. 'I tried to sneak in there. It was upsetting that it [the news] got out. I didn't mean for anyone to get worried about me. I was dehydrated, and my temperature flew, so I had to spend a day in hospital. Everything's fine now.'

Through her mother, Delta pleaded for the attention to be turned back on the athletes. 'She's resting at the moment, but please remember it's about the athletes, it's not about Delta,' said Lea. 'We just hope our team does really well here. These people have worked their whole lives to get here and she is over here to see them and support them.'

Released from hospital, she rested with her mother at the Hilton Athens before stepping out publicly with Mark to enjoy the Olympic Games. He took her on a tour of the Olympic Village, and they attended Petria Thomas's butterfly victory. Smiling again after her hospitalisation, Delta danced in her seat to the bongo drums played by the Australian swimming team and hugged a boxing kangaroo.

The couple attracted enormous attention in Athens because of their celebrity status and their links to Greece. While playing for Australia, Mark said he was thrilled to be competing at the Olympics in a country which meant so much to his family, and he was embraced as a son of Greece during the Games with cries of '*Hellas, Hellas*'. 'It is always a great joy to have one of the Greeks of the diaspora come to Athens to compete,' says Antonia Moskos. 'I don't know Mark, but I think it would be special.'

Delta also found a huge new fan base. 'She was a star in Athens,' says Stephen Harmon. 'The Greeks loved her, because of her name.' Delta is the fourth letter of the Greek alphabet.

Delta was due to return to London to continue working on her album, but her love for Mark and need to rest made her postpone her return to work until he completed his matches in Athens.

However, while Mark had high hopes of triumphing at the Games after his previous lack of form, he crashed out of the first round of his Olympic tennis match to unseeded Belgian, Olivier Rochas. He 'thundered like Zeus' in the first set, only to dramatically falter. Bitterly disappointed, Mark sighed that he had tendonitis and had felt no power on the ball. 'It's extremely disappointing. You're representing your country, the Olympics are once every four years and I was looking forward to it.'

"I knew it had to be deeper and darker. I wanted my album to be big, dramatic and truthful, because that's how my year has been."

Delta

Delta recording her video clip, *Mistaken Identity*

Delta signing autographs for her fans at Channel [V]

Mark left the next day to prepare for the US Open, missing the wild and glamorous parties organised by sponsors. His quick departure after his crushing performance only led to more speculation about the run of losses. 'Mark flew out of Greece with girlfriend Delta Goodrem last night after a whirlwind few days in Athens,' wrote journalist Leo Schlink. 'He marched at the Opening Ceremony, made a mercy dash to be alongside Delta in hospital, bought souvenirs, wore a holiday-style beach hat around the city and signed scores of autographs for starstruck fans. But neither the grand nature of the occasion, nor the goodwill surrounding his liaison with the Aussie pop star, could inspire Philippoussis on the tennis court . . .'

Delta knew that people wondered if her collapse had once again distracted Mark, but she tried to rise above it. 'It is hard though,' she said once of the constant scrutiny of their relationship and his performance. 'I want the best for Mark and his tennis, so of course it hurts.'

Delta left Athens voicing her support for her embattled boyfriend and her love for him, despite their world schedule forcing frequent separations. 'It's definitely long distance. I have to get back to London to keep working on the album, but I'll hopefully get to see him at one of his games. It's so wonderful that Mark's here playing for Australia,' she said loyally.

Yes, she was a patriotic girl, and even with her improved health enabling her to turn her eyes once again on the US, she would never forget what was in her heart — until it was broken, once again.

"She makes heads turn. Which is quite something in LA, where people would rather steal a handbag than steal a look."

Jean Kittson

CHAPTER 14

America

The LA skyline shimmering behind her, Delta leans against the luxurious leather upholstery of a classic American car. Her skin is lightly tanned, her eyes shine with a knowing glint and her clothes are feminine and stylish. Delta is no longer an innocent and breezy girl. She is a woman, sure of talent and fame, in love, and ready once more to fulfil her ultimate dream: America.

Her new look is sultry and sophisticated. But most of all, to the delight of her friends, she is glowing once more. She exudes the inner beauty that so captivates everyone who meets her. The pictures on her website have also been updated. The young and fresh long blonde curls and butterflies have been replaced with sleek black-and-white pictures that show her new sophistication. Yet her smile, which Delta says is such a special part of who she is, is still only a second away.

'I know people are talking about her new look. But I don't see it, I think because I have seen it gradually evolve,' says Stephen Harmon. However, even he is struck by the way Delta looks now. 'She looks stunning at the moment. Just beautiful,' says Stephen. 'I once saw her come out of a swimming pool and I thought, Oh! She was so ravishing. It's not just physical beauty. It is her aura. But I've seen her with no hair and I still felt that.'

When Jean Kittson, Delta's co-star on *Hating Alison Ashley*, met Delta in LA with photographer James Houston for *OK!* magazine, Jean was struck by Delta's glamorous surroundings — she was staying at the Philippe Starck-designed Standard Hotel — but says that, amongst so much consciously sleek style and perfumed posing, Delta stood out all the more for her natural beauty and warmth. 'She makes heads turn,' Jean observed during her days with Delta. 'Which is quite something in LA, where people would rather steal a handbag than steal a look.'

For Delta, all her feelings about this new chapter in her life and her renewed health and happiness were summed up in her song, *Out of the Blue*. Knowing her new album had a darker mood, Delta chose *Out of the Blue* as her comeback song because it was the most 'hopeful'. 'I knew straight away it had to be the first single,' Delta said on the eve of the song's release. 'I think it's perfect because it's saying, I'm still here, I'm still singing, I want to enjoy the fact I'm out of the blue and back into the world.'

As she becomes a global superstar she continues to reach out and relate to her audience through her song writing. She continues to remind fans how much she cares about her 'friends'.

Yet Delta has to reconcile her need for privacy in her new international celebrity world with her instinctive autobiographical song writing, which releases her deepest feelings. She was forced to confront an embarrassing and scandalous end to her relationship with Mark Philippoussis right in the middle of promoting the song about her love for him — *Out of the Blue*.

The news that Delta and Mark had split would have been widely publicised anyway and hotly speculated upon. But the fact that another celebrity was believed to be involved (and that the break-up came on the heels of Lleyton Hewitt and Kim Clijsters' sudden split) sent the story spinning across the globe.

Rumours first began circulating in the lead-up to the ARIAs. Delta and Mark had not been seen together for some weeks, and she had been working in Sydney promoting her single, *Out of the Blue*, launching a new underwear range and preparing for singing *Out of the Blue* at the ARIAs. 'I just want to put on a good performance, that's really my focus this year,' she said. 'I just want to perform and sing for people.

'This year's ARIAs — it's weird going back,' she added. 'It's like my illness never happened.' Delta firmly assured everyone she was still with Mark, but later admitted, 'I think he's playing tennis somewhere.' It was a telling sign, and celebrity watchers were intrigued, wondering if Mark would be escorting her to the ARIAs.

Delta had already learnt that where there was a hit, there was a writ. Now she was about to receive another celebrity life lesson: where there was a tennis player, there was Paris Hilton.

Delta appeared at the ARIAs alone, in an exquisite gold and white dress. If she had already split with Mark, as he later claimed, she was hiding her heartbreak behind a professional smile on the red carpet. Her performance that night was later criticised as 'tuneless', causing speculation that the couple had split — there had been mysterious sightings of him with another woman — and that her emotional upset had put her performance off.

'Not true,' a friend says loyally. 'Delta was nervous, that was all. It was a huge night for her. She is too professional to allow her feelings to affect her performance.'

It was noted that she didn't thank Mark when she received her ARIA that night. If Delta was hoping to keep the split quiet until she had finished promoting *Out of the Blue*, her hopes would be in vain. Instead, a week after the ARIAs, Australia woke to the news that Paris Hilton claimed Mark was her new love. She told two astounded Australian tourists on a shopping tour with her, 'I've got a new man, and I'm head over heels in love.' The 23-year-old heiress was quoted as saying, 'I adore him, he's hot. His name is Mark Philippoussis.' Adding insult to injury, Paris said Mark dumped Delta because she was 'boring'.

"I don't know if she will make it in the US. She's a Celine Dion type, and that's not what is big on the market there at the moment. To make it in the US is very, very tough — and you need your record company pushing like hell."

A music industry insider

It appeared Mark the playboy was back, and the sins of Delta's ex-boyfriend Jay Till were forgotten in the rush to find out the truth of the scandal. Was Mark — the man her mother had said sprinkled fairy dust when Delta was at her lowest moment — now the biggest Love Rat of them all?

In London to promote *Out of the Blue* and film a video clip of her duet with Brian McFadden, Delta was horrified at being dragged into such an undignified mess, and heartbroken as speculation intensified about Mark's alleged infidelity.

In an interview with radio announcer Alan Jones, Mark denied a fling with Paris but admitted meeting her through ex-girlfriend Tara Reid, not Holly Valance as first thought. He said Paris was just a friend and pleaded that he had done the honourable thing and rung Delta four days before the ARIA awards to end the relationship, as he had to concentrate on tennis. Their two careers had forced them apart, as Delta was not content to trail Mark around the tennis court and Mark was not yet happy to be a pop star's gorgeous tennis player handbag. 'Delta and I had something special,' he said, denying he ever called her boring. 'She's only going to get bigger and I need to concentrate on my tennis.'

It's thought that Delta began to realise her fairytale romance was over when Mark failed to return her text messages and phone calls. He eventually called to end the relationship.

A friend of Mark's later quoted him as saying that splitting with Delta made him 'feel like s**t' and she had cried out 'Why?' when he called her. Mark had said, 'There was no one else involved — I hadn't met Paris. I was speaking from the heart, and my heart told me it wasn't going to work.'

According to those around her, Delta's world collapsed

because she had 'worshipped the ground Mark walked on'. 'I really feel for her,' says a friend. 'She gets her heart broken because she's attracted to these glamorous men, but she's too young to handle them.'

Delta refused to comment at first, and her Sony spokeswoman said bluntly, 'I imagine she wants to crawl under a rock right now.' She later released a statement on her website confirming the split and wishing him all the best. It was classic Delta dignity. Just like other crises in her life, Delta put on a brave front while filming her video with McFadden, sparking more speculation about the nature of her friendship with him.

But privately she sunk to the depths in her mother's arms. Lea had flown straight from Australia to the UK to be with her daughter when the Paris scandal broke. It was seen by some as a cynical move to gather extra publicity if they had already broken up, but with a worldwide scandal breaking over her daughter's head, a private heartbreak had become public humiliation. Any girl would want her mother at such a time.

New Idea quoted a friend of Paris's, Alicia Raines, about the attraction between Mark and Paris: 'Mark didn't know what had hit him,' Raines told journalist Peter Kent. 'Paris was out at a birthday bash and on the prowl. She caught a glimpse of Mark and said, "Ooh, who's that?"'

'Paris didn't waste any time,' another guest revealed to Kent. 'She was wearing a see-through pink dress and her cleavage was on show. When they were introduced, she offered her hand and said, "I'm Paris. Wanna party?"' Alicia claimed the two were locked in Paris's penthouse for 48 hours, but Mark continues to insist that nothing happened and he would never hurt Delta.

"An artist like Delta should travel well. She's pop, a young, lovely attractive woman with an extraordinary story. If this record doesn't work globally, **it won't be for lack of trying."**

Andrew Lack
Head of Sony BMG

Such was the intense interest in the days after news of the split broke that even the *Sydney Morning Herald* could not resist a cartoon. An umpire presiding over a tennis match calls from his chair, 'Wait! This game cannot proceed until we know why you, Mr Philippoussis, broke up with the lovely Ms Goodrem . . .'

Mark's family and friends were aghast at the negative press. His father, Nick, darkly blamed 'Delta's mother and co.' for generating the negative press against his son. But the mere association of Mark with Paris was enough to vilify him without any help from Delta's family, regardless of Mark's repeated claims that they were only friends and he'd already split from Delta before meeting the heiress. There were also reports of an erotic dancer, Brooke Tigh, trying to sell details of her meeting with Mark in California. Negotiations were being handled by her production company, Bad Girl Productions, but the story never appeared. The Scud was clearly shocked at the volley of hate mail directed towards him, especially on Delta's website. His own website banned all mention of the incident and deleted hate mail.

But would the criticism and venom have been so harsh if Mark had been at the top of his game? Shane Warne overcame sordid scandals and a drug charge to be forgiven once he helped Australia clinch victories on the cricket field. The Canterbury Bulldogs swept dark allegations of sexual assault under the carpet with their NRL grand final victory. But Mark was losing games, and he had broken the heart of a young star who had overcome cancer. He was now just a playboy and a cad, not a naughty tennis star.

'He messed with Australia's princess,' says a well-known agent. 'Because of his image now — and his performances — no sponsor will touch him until he wins. But give the guy a break — he didn't kill anyone.'

'If it is true, then Paris and Mark deserve each other,' says a friend of Delta's, horrified by the way the relationship ended. 'He is a womaniser and she is a man-eater.'

As if to prove the point, Paris then provided another twist in the tale by being seen with US tennis star Andy Roddick in Vegas. A tennis insider blames Paris for dragging Mark — and other tennis players like Roddick — into the tabloids. 'The boys (tennis stars!) have all been warned to stay away from her. Mark broke up with Delta before being seen with Paris. At least he had the sense to stay in a group with her so there are no photos of them together, but Andy got caught out as he was photographed alone. They were both bitten . . . and not in a way they'd enjoy being bitten!'

As for Delta, she must now put the heartache and indignity behind her, if only for the sake of her delicate health. 'The heartbreak of losing Mark and the pressure of the accompanying publicity may seriously affect Delta's psychological and emotional wellbeing,' says psychologist Melanie Price.

But the fight for her life has also made Delta realise her strength and spirit. Her journey has taken her on an arc of discovery, romance, betrayal, success and trauma. Yet the little girl inside lives on and she knows so much more because of what she has endured. Her life experience can help her overcome the heartbreak over Mark. She couldn't control Mark's heart, but she can control her own and her destiny in America.

All her decisions seem to now have US links and Stephen Harmon believes she will soon be in a Hollywood film. 'She will go worldwide. She will make America,' he says. She has starred with Beyoncé and Pink in the Pepsi commercial, a massive US company that promotes American stars. She agreed to Australian tourism advertisements that for now are being shown in New Zealand, but if she has success in the US, will no doubt be shown there.

She has a US manager, DC Music, and crucially, the support of her record company, which believes she has the talent and tenacity to become a huge star. She will soon release a debut album in the US, believed to be a mix of her hits from *Innocent Eyes* and her new material on her follow-up album, *Mistaken Identity*.

But a music insider wonders if the market in the US is right at the moment for Delta's style. 'I don't know if she will make it in the US. She's a Celine Dion type, and that's not what is big on the market there at the moment. To make it in the US is very, very tough — and you need your record company pushing like hell.'

Andrew Lack, head of the giant Sony BMG conglomerate, plans to push. He heard Delta in a special showcase for him and said he was so stunned that he planned to turn the Australian sensation into a global superstar. 'An artist like Delta should travel well. She's pop, a young, lovely attractive woman with an extraordinary story. If this record doesn't work globally, it won't be for lack of trying.'

Ron Wilson believes Delta will make it in the US. 'We are only seeing the early stages. She is still so young and I think she will be the greatest star this country has ever produced. I just hope she doesn't forget Australia.' As well as the US, Delta has her eyes on Latin America and has already recorded *Born To Try* in flawless Spanish.

Delta will not be content until she has America listening too. 'I'd like to give my music the best chance it can over here. Australia will always be my home. It's where everyone embraced my music. And I was very fortunate. But I'd love to travel and take it to the rest of the world. We've had a lot of success in Europe and the UK, but I think it would be great to stay in America. You only live once. So I think, you may as well give life your best shot.'

But Delta says reports that she was moving to America were wrong and upsetting. She chose to film her *Out of the Blue* film clip in Malibu. It showcased her sultry new look and reinforced her new focus on the American market. The clip went to air for the first time during her final episodes of *Neighbours* as Nina Tucker provided a potent reminder of how far her journey had taken her since those exciting days as an unknown on the Ramsay Street set.

Like Kylie, Elle and Nicole, Delta now doesn't need a surname. This will be her twenty-first year, and she has joined the AAA list. She was described as the closest thing to royalty now in Australia (until Australia's princess, Mary Donaldson). She is already overwhelmed with the constant attention of photographers. 'She gets tired of it,' says a friend.

In a sign of her growing super-stardom, Delta is now a brand, having, like Kylie Minogue and Elle Macpherson, signed to an underwear company. 'When you have a great bra and undies underneath, it just gives you that take-off-your-clothes feeling, not that I do that,' Delta said at the launch of the Delta by Annabella underwear range in Sydney in October 2004.

The brand will be first released through US company Kmart but, unlike Kylie and Elle who have both posed in sexy campaigns, Delta instead requested models. 'Delta modelling the underwear was never on the table. She wouldn't even consider it,' says Stephen Harmon, who explains the deal first came up during filming of *Hating Alison Ashley* where Delta met the company on set to discuss the line.

In another canny cross-promotional move, the lingerie was

launched the same week *Out of the Blue* was officially released for sale. 'She was very involved in the product. She wanted it to be supportive and beautiful and for real women. She said no waifs — some of the models in the campaign are size 14 and one model is over 30.'

The 'real person' campaign reflects Delta's values and continuing urge to please her public. In April, Delta posted a quick message on her website apologising for not contributing more often but said things had been 'complicated'. 'I really want everyone to know that while I may not post I am always reading your messages and topics and joining in without you knowing,' Delta wrote, in a warm and personal note. She also asked fans if they thought *Love and Light* would be a good title for her next album. Instead it was called *Mistaken Identity*.

She is heartened too that her battle with cancer has changed — and possibly saved — lives, such as Tom Ryan's, and thinks that it gives meaning to her fame. 'I need to be open about this,' Delta reflects. 'I had the sickness and maybe it happened for a reason . . . so I can help other people. A lot of people go through the same thing. A lot go through much worse. Definitely I look at the cards I have been dealt and think this is an opportunity to be honest, maybe to try and help others so they don't feel alone in what they are going through.'

Incredibly, Delta told Jean Kittson that her Hodgkin's disease was a health 'hiccup', but she knows how much it has changed her as a person. 'I don't think she has really changed — I think she has evolved,' Stephen Harmon says. 'She is still the warm, bubbly person with a smile for everyone.'

But Delta knows that facing cancer will give her a depth of perspective to life that only those who know from their own experience of the disease — and those who lived through it with her — can understand. Others can only glimpse it under her smile.

In the wake of the cancer, the tone of Delta's limited interviews changed. Her few remarks before the exclusive and harrowing tale she told *The Australian Women's Weekly* are a dark indication of the trauma she has endured. Interviewing her for the *Herald Sun* to promote her *Neighbours* return, Darren Devlyn wrote, 'As always, Delta was self-deprecating and polite. But she has a maturity and a sense of perspective that weren't apparent eighteen months ago.'

Those following Delta's career and how she has matured are now intrigued by the complexities of her personality that are emerging for the first time as she reacted to very intense and public conflicts and controversies.

Peter Holmes, music writer for Sydney's *Sunday Telegraph*, commented that 'Goodrem's ubiquity in mainstream media over the past two years is unprecedented in Australian pop music history but she remains relatively unknown. How to reconcile the political Delta, who so blatantly snubbed Wheatley at the 2003 ARIA Awards, with the shy, giggly Delta who nervously waved at fans at the same Awards? The media has been restrained in covering Goodrem over the past two years: she seems like a decent kid, she rates, and she's been crook. It may not last forever.'

She is also at the level of stardom where she can request 'no personal questions' — even when they are relevant. According to an amazed Peter Holmes, Sony UK asked British journalists to interview Delta but not ask about *Out of the Blue*'s lyrics. 'As with her controversial split with manager Glenn Wheatley, however, curiosity about Goodrem's relationship with Philippoussis won't be sated until she talks about it.'

Aside from planning her sold-out Visualise tour — believed to be a huge showcase in the vein of a Kylie extravaganza — Delta is now concentrating on the international market.

There is also talk that Delta needs to stop being so saintly. 'I want her to get angry,' says a fan, exasperated with Delta's dignity and good wishes to Philippoussis after the Paris scandal. 'How could she say "I wish him well" after what happened with Paris?'

In a recent debate about Delta in the *Sydney Morning Herald*, journalist Julie Robotham was just as frustrated. 'Wishing an ex-partner well may be the only dignified recourse for a dumped fifty-something. But if you're barely out of high school and gorgeous, then surely what you do is get trashed and be photographed straddling Robbie Williams in a limo.' To Robbie's disappointment, she is yet to straddle him.

But Delta is learning. She is beginning to speak her mind in interviews, dropping hints about her real feelings.

In December 2004, Delta reflected on the past year in which she had experienced so much. 'There was a lot of betrayal; a lot of people really surprised me. I saw a lot of different colours in people that I had never seen before so I guess that was a big growing experience. I learned a lot from that and from a lot of different things that happened — all the situations, the betrayals, the story of the management, everything.'

Her second album *Mistaken Identity* was released on November 22 and was hugely promoted. The film clip for the title track was a reflection of her journey through fame and cancer. She included her brother Trent in the clip and also three of her best friends from drama school.

As the clock turned over into 2005, Delta described herself as energetic and free. It was a new beginning for her. Echoing her launch pad of *Neighbours* in Australia, Delta began her assault on the US with a guest role in the US soap, *North Shore* – playing an Australian singer. She was starting again with her head full of old and new dreams. She was too young and ambitious to slow down.

It would be wrong to say that Delta wants success in the US because her honeymoon period in Australia is over. She has always dreamed of being No. 1 in America. It would be simplistic to say that she is a victim of the tall poppy syndrome although there is probably truth in that too. While everyone has their critics, Delta has received far more critical acclaim than Kylie Minogue, who did not receive a peer-judged ARIA until years after she became an international star.

In a recent article, Christine Sams commented on Delta's apparent rejection by organisers of Australia's 'coolest' festival, Homebake, that it was a 'symptom of the apparent rock snobbery that pervades Australia's music, despite the charts that show the opposite among listeners'.

After the shock and the ordeal of her cancer, Delta took the time to put love and fun before her work. She found it much harder to control a man's heart than to pen a hit song. 'My heart has gone back into my work, my family and being a twenty-year-old,' Delta said, speaking from the set of *North Shore* in Hawaii to the *Sunday Telegraph*.

After her split with Mark, rumours intensified about the true nature of Delta's relationship with fellow singer Brian McFadden as they filmed the clip of their duet together. A source on set claimed to the UK's *Daily Mirror* that Brian had a soft spot for Delta. At first she would only say they were friends and that 'she knew what it was like to get a cheery phone call when you are down' in relation to their apparently intense phone calls. Like Delta, Brian wore his songs on his sleeve. He sang about his recent divorce from Kerry Katona and living away from his children in a song called *Love Daddy*: 'Unforseen misery has come between your mummy and me.' Both performed in the Royal Variety Concert for Prince Charles in December 2004 and spent time together backstage, according to jazz star Michael Bublé, who met them both with Lea's mum as they waited for their performances.

In January 2005, Delta was suddenly photographed holidaying with Brian McFadden at an exclusive resort in South Africa. At the same time, glamorous beauty Alexis Barbara appeared court-side to support Mark Philippoussis in Perth. Was it a planned move or coincidence that Delta revealed her new love at the same time as Mark revealed his in Australia? What is certain is that, despite the repeated denials, it appears there was romance with McFadden all along. 'Sad but true,' said radio identity Kyle Sandilands when asked if the new romance was genuine.

Delta's innate Scorpian strength, often previously overshadowed by her sweetness, is now more apparent, and she seems frustrated sometimes that some people can't see how much she has changed. With the new album revealing the truth once more, perhaps people will hear the difference in her rather than see it as skin deep.

'I have this idea that people look at me and think that, aside from the short hair, I am the same person, the same Delta,' she says. 'It's as though they are just waiting for my hair to grow back and I will be the same again, as though nothing has happened. But you can't go through something like this and be the same person at the end. It's simply not possible.'

Dr Phyllis Butow agrees Delta will always feel the impact of cancer, although that may not necessarily be a negative experience. 'Fear of death is an obvious issue. Most people describe this as an existential crisis. Those who experience cancer have a very different awareness of time, and of their own vulnerability. That doesn't go away at the end of treatment. They have a heightened awareness of death and there is something of a barrier between them and their peer group. They feel nobody understands them.

'They sense that they now are operating on a different time frame and have different priorities. Delta will feel particularly out of step with her peers. While most people adjust well, it is a common experience to feel no longer the same person. Delta now has a cancer identity.'

For a complex person such as Delta, with intense ties to her family and her fans, and a need to please and succeed, her story will continually surprise. Time is going to show if Delta becomes the global enduring star, like Olivia, that she dreamed of as a child. She is nearly there, but this is also only her twenty-first year.

Her 'hiccup' was a dramatic reminder of the need to balance success with serenity, and awards and achievements with love and life. Yet Delta's driven personality and perfectionism will only push her harder to the stars.

'I love performing. I do this so I can get up and sing for people. It's a big world and there's so much to do. I have a lot of goals. I want to take my music to people and tell my story, perhaps one day be singing at the ARIAs and the Brits and the Grammys. Just world domination — I'm not asking for much.'

With such a driven and restless personality, will Delta, for all her beautiful warmth of heart, ever be truly happy?

'I've got mixed feelings,' sighs a friend. 'I think . . .' She stops and reflects on what she is about to say. Then her thoughts become clear. 'Delta has attained an amazing life and success and I really hope she finds the happiness she deserves.'

ACKNOWLEDGEMENTS

The author would like to thank the following people for their advice, assistance with research, and encouragement:

Richard Walsh, Andrea McNamara, Kevin Airs, Angela Mollard, Nigel Wright, Tracy Schaverien, Rick Maier and Jane Worthington. Thanks also to all those people who agreed to be interviewed for this book.

PICTURE CREDITS

In order of appearance:

With a temporary tattoo on her shoulder, proclaiming her love of Melbourne. 18/11/2002 Photographer: Craig Wood/NEWSPIX

With Sydney Swans player Jude Bolton, arriving at the *Vanilla Sky* movie premiere. 19/12/2001
Photographer: John Stanton/GETTY IMAGES

As Nina on the *Neighbours* set. 21/03/2003
Photographer: Rob Baird/NEWSPIX

With Blair at the 2002 Bastille Day Ball.
Photographer: Serge Thomann

Celebrating her first No. 1 hit with the *Neighbours* cast, 2002.
Photographer: Serge Thomann

With Glenn Wheatley and his wife Gaynor at the Logies.
28/04/2002 Photographer: Cameron Tandy/NEWSPIX

Delta and Blair McDonough in a fashion shoot for *Girlfriend*.
06/2002 Photographer: Fabrizio
Lipardi/LIZARD MANAGEMENT

At the 2003 Logies. Photographer: Serge Thomann

Performing at the 2003 Alan Border Medal.
Photographer: Serge Thomann

Arriving at the 17th Annual ARIA awards in Sydney with her mother Lea, father Dennis and younger brother Trent. 21/10/2003
Photographer: John Stanton/GETTY IMAGES

With Mark Philippoussis in Bondi. 16/01/2004
Photographer: Jeff Darmanin/NEWSPIX

With Mark Philippoussis at the 2004 Logies.
Photographer: Serge Thomann

With Lea at the 2002 Bastille Day Ball.
Photographer: Serge Thomann

In concert, Christmas 2002.Photographer: Serge Thomann

Paul Higgins in Studio 52 in Melbourne where the first recordings of Delta (shown on screen) were made when she was 14.
17/10/2003 Photographer: David Geraghty/NEWSPIX

Performing with Brian McFadden at the Royal Variety Performance, Coliseum, London. 13/12/2004
Photographer: Rex Features/AUSTRAL

Recording her new video clip *Mistaken Identity* in Sydney.
26/11/2004 Photographer: Jeff Darmanin/NEWSPIX

Signing autographs for her fans during *What U Want* at Channel [V] Fox Studios, Sydney. 12/11/2004
Photographer: John Stanton/GETTY IMAGES

At Melbourne airport arriving back home. 9/11/2004
Photographer: Ian Currie/NEWSPIX

On the set of *Hating Alison Ashley*. 10/05/2004
Photographer: Mark Smith/NEWSPIX

"I don't think she really **has changed** — I think she **has evolved.** She is still the **warm, bubbly person** with a smile for **everyone.**"

Stephen Harmon
Delta's theatrical agent

Delta at Melbourne airport arriving back home

Delta on the set of *Hating Alison Ashley*